THE
SALVATION
OF ALL

THE
SALVATION
OF ALL

Creation's Final Destination
(A Biblical Look at Universal Reconciliation)

Clyde L. Pilkington, Jr.

BIBLE STUDENT'S PRESS™
Windber, Pennsylvania

Original Printing:
Individual articles published in the *Bible Student's Notebook*™, 2005-2006

Second Printing:
First book edition, 2007

Third Printing:
Second book edition, 2009

Fourth Printing:
Third book edition, 2010

Executive Editor: Andre Sneidar
Layout and Design: Great Adventure in Faith

Cover design by Clyde L. Pilkington, III
Cover photograph by Clyde L. Pilkington, III
(Just off of Lincoln Highway, Rt. 30, near the former location of S.S. Grand View Ship Hotel, Schellsburg, Pennsylvania)

   ISBN-10:   1-934251-01-1
   ISBN-13:   978-1-934251-01-0

Published by:
Bible Student's Press™
An imprint of *Pilkington & Sons*
P.O. Box 265
Windber, PA 15963
1-800-784-6010

For information on *Bible Student's Press*™ releases, visit
   www.BibleStudentsPress.com

For information on other Bible study resources, visit
   www.StudyShelf.com

Printed in the United States of America.

Dedicated to …

The members of Christ's Body who, over the past two millennia, have, in spite of opposition and trial, faithfully carried out their ambassadorship, outside of the religious system.

CONTENTS

INTRODUCTION

Dear Saints,

The Gospel of our Lord and Saviour Jesus Christ is truly better "good news" than we could ever have imagined! It is far more glorious than organized religion would ever have us believe!

It is with great joy that I share with you the wonderful truths related to our theme, The Salvation of All. They represent years of personal study, and I trust that they will prove to be enlightening and encouraging to you.

The chapters are designed to be brief and to the point, sharing as simply as possible the blessed truths that have come to be so important to me.

It was not until I finally broke all ties with all organized religion that my heart was free to really enjoy and embrace this marvelous message. I trust that you too will be at liberty to set aside traditional paradigms and enjoy these amazing riches of Christ's finished cross-work!

Study to show yourself approved unto God, a workman that needs not to be ashamed, rightly dividing the Word of Truth (II Timothy 2:15).

Prove all things; hold fast that which is good (I Thessalonians 5:21).

For the love of God, and His truth,

Your fellow,

Clyde

Clyde L. Pilkington, Jr.

Who will have all men to be saved, and to come to the knowledge of the truth.

~ I Timothy 2:4

Chapter 1

THE SALVATION *OF* ALL

Grace is much more glorious and amazing than man recognizes. Religion hides the full accomplishments of the vast cross-work of the Lord Jesus Christ. The work of salvation for mankind is full and complete. As ambassadors of Christ, we are only to proclaim its glorious message. Those who respond by faith can enjoy their salvation in Christ now while here on earth.

Make no mistake about it. When I speak of salvation, I do not just speak of the *potential* of "salvation *for* all" – in the sense that it is only available *for* all men to have; but I speak freely of the *surety* of the "salvation *of* all" – that all men will in reality enjoy the fullness of salvation, completely applied to them personally.

I firmly believe in the *salvation of all* – that God in His goodness, grace, and love, on the account of the cross-work redemption of the Lord Jesus Christ, will indeed actually save *all* mankind.

There are three different views of the destiny of the lost. These approaches can be termed as (1) "Eternal Conscious Torment," (2) "Annihilation," (3) "Universal Reconciliation." All three have *apparent* scriptural support, but for *every* verse apparently supporting the first two views, there are many more verses that appear to support the latter.

According to theology, the majority of God's creation will be hopelessly lost to Him. It teaches that God knowingly (with foreknowledge) created mankind, the majority of which He will eternally damn. However, this is out of character with the true God of the Scriptures.

Here are examples of verses that show the salvation of all mankind:

> And I will make of you a great nation, and I will bless you, and make your name great; and you shalt be a blessing: and I will bless them who bless you, and curse him who curses you: and in you shall **all families** of the earth be blessed (Genesis 12:2-3).

> **All the ends of the world** shall remember and turn to the LORD: and **all the kindreds** of the nations shall worship before You (Psalm 22:27).

> The LORD is merciful and gracious, slow to anger, **and plenteous in mercy.** He will **not always chide:** neither will He keep His anger forever. He has not dealt with us after our sins; nor rewarded us according to our iniquities (Psalm 103:8-10).

> And it shall come to pass in the last days, that the mountain of the LORD'S house shall be established in the top of the mountains, and shall be exalted above the hills; and **all nations** shall flow unto it (Isaiah 2:2).

> Every valley shall be filled, and every mountain and hill shall be brought low; and the crooked shall be made straight, and the rough ways shall be made smooth; And **all flesh** shall see the salvation of God (Luke 3:5, 6).

> That was the true Light [Jesus Christ], Who lights **every man** who comes into the world (John 1:9).

> The next day John sees Jesus coming to him, and says, "Behold the Lamb of God, Who takes away the **sin of the world"** (John 1:29).

> … This is indeed the Christ, **the Savior of the world** (John 4:42).

> And I, if I be lifted up from the earth, will draw **all men** unto Me (John 12:32).

> Whom the heaven must receive until the times of **restitution of all things,**

which God has spoken by the mouth of all His holy prophets since the world began (Acts 3:21).

*For if by one man's offence death reigned by one; much more they who receive abundance of grace and of the gift of righteousness shall reign in life by One, Jesus Christ. Therefore as by the offence of one judgment came upon **all men** to condemnation; even so by the righteousness of One the free gift came **upon all men** unto justification of life. For as by one man's disobedience many were made sinners, so by the obedience of One shall many be made righteous* (Romans 5:17-19).

*For as you in times past have not believed God, yet have now obtained mercy through their unbelief: even so have these also now not believed, that through your mercy they also may obtain mercy. For God has concluded them all in unbelief, that He might have **mercy upon all**. O the depth of the riches both of the wisdom and knowledge of God! how unsearchable are His judgments, and His ways past finding out! For who has known the mind of the Lord? or who has been His counsellor? Or who has first given to Him, and it shall be recompensed to him again? For of Him, and through Him, and to Him, are **all things:** to Whom be glory for ever. Amen* (Romans 11:30-36).

*For since by man came death, by man came also the resurrection of the dead. For as in Adam **all die,** even so in Christ shall **all be made alive.** But **every man** in his own order: Christ the firstfruits; afterward they who are Christ's at His coming. Then comes the end, when He shall have delivered up the kingdom to God, even the Father; when He shall have put down all rule and all authority and power. For He must reign, until He has put all enemies under His feet. The last enemy that shall be destroyed is death. For He has put all things under His feet. But when He says all things are put under Him, it is manifest that He is excepted, Who did put all things under Him. And when all things shall be subdued unto Him, then shall the Son also Himself be subject unto Him Who put **all things** under Him, that God may be **All in all*** (I Corinthians 15:21-28).

*For the love of Christ constrains us; because we thus judge, that if One died for **all,** then were all dead … To wit, that God was in Christ, **reconciling the world** to Himself, not imputing their trespasses unto them; and has committed unto us the Word of reconciliation* (II Corinthians 5:14, 19).

*That in the dispensation of the fulness of times He might gather together in one **all things** in Christ, both which are in heaven, and which are on earth; even in Him* (Ephesians 1:10).

*And, having made peace through the blood of His cross, by Him to reconcile **all things** to Himself; by Him, I say, whether they be things in earth, or things in heaven* (Colossians 1:20).

*Who gave Himself a **ransom for all,** to be testified in due time* (I Timothy 2:6).

*For therefore we both labor and suffer reproach, because we trust in the living God, Who is the **Savior of all men,** especially of those who believe* (I Timothy 4:10).

*And He is the propitiation for our sins: and not for ours only, but also for he sins of the **whole world*** (I John 2:2).

*And God shall wipe away all tears from their eyes; and there shall be no more death, neither sorrow, nor crying, neither shall there be any more pain: for the former things are **passed away*** (Revelation 21:4).

Even Sodom, the great example of God's wrath and judgment, will not be exempt from the restoration of God's Love.

*"And your elder sister is Samaria, she and her daughters who dwell at your left hand: and your younger sister, who dwells at your right hand, is Sodom and her daughters. Yet have you not walked after their ways, nor done after their abominations: but, as if that were a very little thing, you were corrupted more than they in all your ways. As I live," says the Lord GOD, "Sodom your sister has not done, she nor her daughters, as you have done, you and your daughters. ... When I shall bring again their captivity, the captivity of Sodom and her daughters, and the captivity of Samaria and her daughters, then will I bring again the captivity of your captives in the midst of them: ... When your sisters, Sodom and her daughters, shall return to their former estate, and Samaria and her daughters **shall return to their former estate,** then you and your daughters shall return to your former estate"* (Ezekiel 16:46-48, 53, 55).

Praise the Lord! He is the Lord of both the dead and the living.

For to this end Christ both died, and rose, and revived, that He might be Lord both of the dead and living (Romans 14:9).

It is God's will that *all* men are saved:

*Who will have **all men** to be saved, and to come unto the knowledge of the truth. For there is one God, and One mediator between God and men, the Man Christ Jesus; Who gave Himself a **ransom for all,** to be testified in due time* (I Timothy 2:4-6).

God accomplishes *all* that He wills to do:

But He is in one mind, and who can turn Him? and what His soul desires, even that He does" (Job 23:13).

For I know that the LORD is great, and that our Lord is above all gods. Whatsoever the LORD pleased, that did He in heaven, and in earth, in the seas, and all deep places (Psalms 135:5-6).

*Declaring the end from the beginning, and from ancient times the things that are not yet done, saying, "My counsel shall stand, and **I will do all My pleasure"*** (Isaiah 46:10).

*In Whom also we have obtained an inheritance, being predestinated according to the purpose of Him **Who works all things after the counsel of His Own will*** (Ephesians 1:11).

The Lord Jesus Christ taught His followers to love their enemies. He revealed that this was the very nature of the Father:

But I say to you, Love your enemies, bless them who curse you, do good to them who hate you, and pray for them who despitefully use you, and persecute you; that you may be the children of your Father Who is in heaven: for He makes His sun to rise on the evil and on the good, and sends rain on the just and on the unjust. For if you love them who love you, what reward have you? Do not even the publicans the same? And if you salute your brothers only, what do you do more than others? Do not even the publicans so? Be therefore perfect, even as your Father Who is in heaven is perfect (Matthew 5:44-48).

God is love:

He who loves not knows not God; for God is love. In this was manifested the love of God toward us, because that God sent His only begotten Son into the world, that we might live through Him. Herein is love: not that we loved God, but that He loved us, and sent His Son to be the propitiation for our sins (I John 4:8-10).

How excellent is Your lovingkindness… (Psalm 36:7).

But God, Who is rich in mercy, for His great love wherewith He loved us, even when we were dead in sins … (Ephesians 2:4-5).

But God commends His love toward us, in that, while we were yet sinners, Christ died for us (Romans 5:8).

But after that the kindness and love of God our Savior toward man appeared (Titus 3:4).

God is love … (I John 4:16).

We have the assurance of God that love *never* fails:

Charity never fails (I Corinthians 13:8).

To fail is the translation of *ekpipto* (ek-pip'-to, Greek #1601), from G1537 and G4098, "to drop away; specially, be driven out of one's course; figuratively, to lose, become inefficient." It is also translated as – *"be cast," "fall"* (*away, off*), and *"take none effect."*[1]

All creation shall be freed from the bondage of vanity and corruption:

*For the earnest expectation of the creature waits for the manifestation of the sons of God. For the creature was made subject to vanity, not willingly, but by reason of Him Who has subjected the same in hope, because **the creature** itself also **shall be delivered** from the bondage of corruption into the glorious liberty of the children of God. For we know that **the whole creation** groans and travails in pain together until now* (Romans 8:19-22).

---

1. James Strong, *The Exhaustive Concordance of the Bible.*

All of the Lord's works shall praise Him, and He will raise up *all* who are bowed down:

*The LORD is gracious, and full of compassion; slow to anger, and of great mercy. The LORD is good to **all:** and His tender mercies are over **all** His works. **All Your works** shall praise You, O LORD; and Your saints shall bless You ... The LORD upholds **all** who fall, and raises up **all** those who are bowed down (Psalms 145:8-10, 14).*

All shall bow down:

*Look unto Me, and be saved, **all** the ends of the earth: for I am God, and there is none else. I have sworn by Myself, the word is gone out of My mouth in righteousness, and shall not return, that unto Me **every** knee shall bow, **every** tongue shall swear (Isaiah 45:22-23).*

*That at the name of Jesus **every** knee should bow, of things in heaven, and things in earth, and things under the earth; and that **every** tongue should confess that Jesus Christ is Lord, **to the glory** of God the Father (Philippians 2:10-11).*

This confession is the *work* of the Holy Spirit:

*Wherefore I give you to understand, that no man speaking by the Spirit of God calls Jesus accursed: and that **no man** can say that Jesus is the Lord, but by the Holy Spirit (I Corinthians 12:3).*

Therefore, *every* creature will praise the Lord:

*And **every creature** which is in heaven, and on the earth, and under the earth, and such as are in the sea, and **all** that are in them, heard I saying, "Blessing, and honor, and glory, and power, be to Him Who sits upon the throne, and to the Lamb for ever and ever" (Revelation 5:13).*

"The Love of God"

The Love of God is greater far
    Than tongue or pen can ever tell
It goes beyond the highest star
    And reaches to the lowest hell

The guilty pair, bowed down with care
    God gave His Son to win
His erring child He reconciled
    And pardoned from his sin.

Could we with ink the ocean fill
    And were the skies of parchment made
Were every stalk on earth a quill
    And every man a scribe by trade

To write the Love of God above
    Would drain the ocean dry
Nor could the scroll contain the whole
    Though stretched from sky to sky.

Oh Love of God, How rich and pure!
    How measureless and strong!
It shall forever more endure
    The saint's and angel's song.

~ Frederick M. Lehman, 1917

The only victory love can enjoy is the day when its offer of love is answered by the return of love. The only possible final triumph is a universe loved by God and in love with God.[2]

---

2. *William Barclay: A Spiritual Autobiography,* 1977, William Barclay (1907-1978), page 67.

For the wages of sin is death; but the gift of God is
eternal life through Jesus Christ our Lord.

~ Romans 6:23

Chapter 2

THE WAGES OF SIN

The Scripture is very plain as to the penalty of sin:

For the wages of sin is death (Romans 6:23).

Contemporary Christianity still has not shaken off the Roman, Dark-age superstition that the penalty of sin is eternal conscious torment of the wicked in hell.

Tradition would have us believe that Romans 6:23 really means "the wages of sin is eternal conscious torment in fiery hell." Nonetheless, the Scriptures say that the penalty is death.

In fact, if the penalty of sin is eternal conscious torment of the wicked in hell, then Christ cannot be the Saviour of the world, for He has not made such a payment for sin.

Christ *is* the Saviour of the world, and He did make the full and complete payment for sin. He did so by dying for the sins of the world.

Christ died for our sins according to the Scriptures (I Corinthians 15:3).

Who His Own self bore our sins in His Own body on the tree (I Peter 2:24).

THE GRAVE

All men go to the same place.

For that which befalls the sons of men befalls beasts; even one thing befalls them: as the one dies, so dies the other; yea, they have all one breath; so that a man has no preeminence above a beast: for all is vanity. All go to one place; all are of the dust, and all turn to dust again (Ecclesiastes 3:19-20).

The dead are not in heaven.

And no man has ascended up to heaven, but He Who came down from heaven, even the Son of man Who is in heaven (John 3:13).

Men and brothers, let me freely speak to you of the patriarch David, that he is both dead and buried, and his sepulcher is with us to this day. ... For David is not ascended into the heavens (Acts 2:29, 34).

Death does not take one to be with the Lord. Death is an enemy *("the last enemy that shall be destroyed is death"* – I Corinthians 15:26). The only way believers can go to heaven and be with the Lord is for Him to return and get them at His coming.

For the Lord Himself shall descend from heaven ... So shall we ever be with the Lord (I Thessalonians 4:17).

The dead are in their graves.

... All who are in their graves shall hear His voice (John 5:28).

... Them who sleep in the dust shall awake ... (Daniel 12:2).

... You who dwell in the dust ... (Isaiah 26:19).

The dead are always said to be where their bodies are.

... Abraham buried Sarah his wife in the cave of the field of Machpelah ... (Genesis 23:19).

... There was Abraham buried, and Sarah his wife (Genesis 25:10).

So David slept with his fathers, and was buried ... (I Kings 2:10).

Men and brothers, let me freely speak to you of the patriarch David, that he is both dead and buried, and his sepulcher is with us to this day (Acts 2:29).

And Solomon slept with his fathers, and he was buried in the city of David his father ... (II Chronicles 9:31).

And devout men carried Stephen to his burial, and made great lamentation over him (Acts 8:2).

"Death of the body" and "resurrection of the body" are not biblical expressions. Death is the death of the *person*. Resurrection is the resurrection of the *person*. In the Bible it is the *person* that is said to die.

HELL

Eternal conscious torment was a part of the sadistic teaching of Augustine. Hell was a profitable institution for Rome.

Our English word "hell" is the translation of one Hebrew and three Greek words.

Hebrew: *sheol*

Sheol is translated:

> "grave" 32 times
> "hell" 31 times
> "pit" 3 times

Concerning Sheol, E.W. Bullinger has written,

> As to the rendering "hell," it does *not* represent *sheol*, because both by dictionary definition and by colloquial usage "hell" means the place of future *punishment*. *Sheol* has no such meaning, but denotes the *present state of death*. "The grave" is, therefore, a far more suitable translation, because it visibly suggests to us what

is invisible to the mind, *viz.*, the state of death. It must, necessarily, be misleading to the English reader to see the former put to represent the latter.

The student will find that "THE grave," taken literally as well as figuratively, will meet all the requirements of the Hebrew *sheol:* not that *sheol* means so much specifically "A grave," as generically, "THE grave ..."

Sheol therefore means *the state of death;* or the state of the dead, of which the grave is a tangible evidence. ... It may be represented by a coined word, "Grave-dom," as meaning the dominion or power of *the grave.*[1]

Greek: *"hades"*

This Greek word *"hades"* is defined by God.

In the Old Testament, He wrote:

> *For You wilt not leave My soul in hell* [sheol]; *neither will You suffer Your Holy One to see corruption* (Psalms 16:10).

Then in the New Testament, quoting the Psalms He writes:

> *Because You will not leave My soul in hell* [hades], *neither will You suffer Your Holy One to see corruption* (Acts 2:27).

Therefore, God defines the Greek word *"hades"* as the Hebrew word *"sheol."*

Greek: *"gehenna"*

Gehenna was a historical place. It was the dump where Jerusalem burnt its trash. It is used metaphorically of the "removal of your trash."

Greek: *"tartaroo"*

One of the three Greek words translated *"hell"* in the *King James Version* appears only one time. *"Tartaroo"* (English transliteration *"tartarus"*) is Strong's Greek Lexicon #5020, translated *"hell"* in II Peter 2:4.

---

1. E.W. Bullinger, *A Critical Lexicon and Concordance to the English and Greek New Testament,* p. 367.

Peter warned,

"But there were false prophets also among the people, even as there shall be false teachers among you, who privily shall bring in damnable heresies, even denying the Lord that bought them, and bring upon themselves swift destruction" (II Peter 2:1).

Damnable heresies are "heresies of destruction or perdition."

Concerning these things, E.W. Bullinger has written,

The teaching that the punishment of the unrighteous begins at the moment of death is a very serious blot on the justice of God. If this is the truth, then Cain, who died about six thousand years ago has already endured six millenniums of punishment, while another murderer who dies today begins to suffer today. Therefore Cain will have to suffer six thousand years more for the same crime than the murderer who dies today.

If two men charged with identical crimes and equally guilty were sentenced, one for five years and the other for ten years, all men who love justice would cry out against such a miscarriage of justice. Shall we not also cry out against any teaching that insists that one man suffer six thousand years more than another for the identical crime? It is indeed a fearful travesty of truth to teach that men are tortured for their sins before they ever have their day in court, and that later they do have their day in court merely to receive a sentence that is determined beforehand. Would not this make the justice of the great white throne to be of the same character as the justice ordered by a Mexican general who said, "Give the man a fair trial, then shoot him." Can this be the justice of God? Can this be the teaching of the Word of God? Do you know that it is? Are you sure that it is? Or can it be that you just do not care?

The contention that God's holiness is of such nature that His justice can never be satisfied by anything save [except] eternal conscious suffering as the penalty for sins needs to be carefully examined. If this dogma is true, then this is the penalty Christ should have paid when He died for our sins. He paid the debt that we owed to God, but He did not suffer eternally. If the debt we owed was "eternal suffering," then that debt has never been paid. Jesus Christ suffered just six hours on the Cross. He did not suffer eternally.

If we would know of God's wrath against sin, we need to look at the Cross. We will learn from this that our God does punish sin, but we will also learn that the wages of sin is death and not eternal conscious torment.[2]

Speaking of the roots of "hell," Bullinger writes,

This is a heathen word and comes down to us surrounded with heathen traditions, which had their origin in Babel, and not in the Bible, and have reached us through Judaism and Romanism.[3]

2. Cited by Otis Q. Sellers, *The Study of Human Destiny*, 1955, page 17.
3. Bullinger's Lexicon.

Wherefore I take you to record this day, that I am pure from the blood of all men. For I have not shunned to declare unto you all the counsel of God.

~ Acts 20:26-27

Chapter 3

PAUL'S TEACHING ON HELL

Paul has been given a very special place in our age. He has been chosen by God as the Apostle to the Gentiles – to the Nations. He is our divinely appointed Apostle.

For I speak to you Gentiles, inasmuch as I am the apostle of the Gentiles, I magnify my office (Romans 11:13).

God revealed to him alone the distinct message for our day:

• **The Gospel of the Grace of God**

*… The ministry, which I have received of the Lord Jesus, to testify **the Gospel of the Grace of God*** (Acts 20:24).

This gospel was committed to Paul's trust.

*According to the glorious **gospel** of the blessed God, **which was committed to my trust*** (I Timothy 1:11).

Paul calls this distinct gospel given to him by God for us, *"my gospel."*

*In the day when God shall judge the secrets of men by Jesus Christ according to **my gospel** (Romans 2:16).*

*Now to Him who is of power to stablish you according to **my gospel** ... (Romans16:25).*

*But I certify you, brothers, that the gospel which was preached of me is not after man. For I neither received it of man, neither was I taught it, but **by the revelation of Jesus Christ** (Galatians 1:11-12).*

- **The Dispensation of the Grace of God**

  *... **The Dispensation of the Grace of God** which is given me to you-ward"* (Ephesians 3:2).

  *... I am made a minister, according to **the Dispensation of God** which is given to me for you ...* (Colossians 1:25).

- **The Revelation of the Mystery**

  *Now to Him Who is of power to establish you according to my gospel, and the preaching of Jesus Christ, according **to the Revelation of the Mystery, which was kept secret since the world began** (Romans 16:25).*

  *... By revelation He made known unto me **the Mystery** ... (Ephesians 3:2-3).*

God gave these revelations to Paul for us – members of the Church, the Body of Christ:

... The Church, Which is His Body (Ephesians 1:22-23).

... The Body, the Church ... (Colossians 1:18).

Paul is the divinely authorized spokesman of God for this age.

If any man thinks himself to be a prophet, or spiritual, let Him acknowledge that the things that I write unto you are the commandments of the Lord (I Corinthians 14:37).

As C.I. Scofield has stated, "In his [Paul's] writings **alone** we find the **doctrine,** position, walk and destiny of the church" (*Scofield Reference Bible,* Ephesians 3:6, emphasis ours).

This is true, for the Scriptures are clear about the unique message and ministry of Paul:

> *Whereunto He called you by* **our gospel,** *to the obtaining of the glory of our Lord Jesus Christ. Therefore, brothers, stand fast, and hold the traditions which you have been taught, whether* **by word, or our epistle** (II Thessalonians 2:14-15).

> *Hold fast the* **form of sound words***, which you have* **heard of me,** *in faith and love which is in Christ Jesus* (II Timothy 1:13).

> *And the things that you hast* **heard of me** *among many witnesses,* **the same** *commit to faithful men, who shall be able to teach others also* (II Timothy 2:2).

> *Holding fast the* **faithful word** *as he has been taught, that he may be able by sound doctrine both to exhort and to convince the gainsayers* (Titus 1:9).

Because Paul is God's spokesman for us today, we are to study his teaching faithfully when considering the application of any doctrine.

> *Study to show yourself approved unto God, a workman who needs not to be ashamed, rightly dividing the Word of Truth"* (II Timothy 2:15).

The subject of Hell is no exception. What follows in this chapter is a *complete* listing of *every* occurrence of Paul's usage of the word *hell* as recorded in the *King James Version* of the Bible. We shall list all of his teachings regarding hell as recorded by Luke in the *Book of Acts,* as well as himself in all of his epistles (*Romans* through *Philemon*) on the following pages:

Paul's Usage of the Word *"Hell"*

in the

<u>Book of Acts</u>

Paul's Usage of the Word

"Hell" in

<u>His Epistles</u>

Are you surprised to see empty columns?

Did you ever stop to consider that Paul, our Apostle, *never once* used the word "hell"?

He didn't use the word *hell* in any recorded messages from the Book of Acts. He didn't use the word *hell* in any of his epistles. Not once! None! Zero!

How could this possibly be?

How could Paul have conducted a teaching ministry that brought glory to God, and yet never have even once used the word *hell?* Isn't the traditional, orthodox doctrine of *hell* at the very foundation of the religious system's creeds?

How could Paul have been so negligent? How could he have gone through his entire ministry forgetting to use such a crucial word? What's up with that?

Or, is it possible that Paul understood something we don't? Could it be we have been deeply buried under religious tradition?

Consider for a moment this declaration of Paul himself, found in the Book of Acts:

> *Wherefore I take you to record this day, that I am pure from the blood of all men. For I have not shunned to declare unto you **all** the counsel of God* (Acts 20:26-27).

The plain and simple fact is that Paul was NOT negligent in his teaching ministry. Here is a passage that makes this clear. Paul said that he was *"pure from the blood of all men,"* because he had declared *"**all** the counsel of God"* – a counsel which obviously DID NOT include *hell* at all.

Do we find ourselves perplexed that Paul, the Apostle, *never* used the word hell and yet was able to declare *"all the counsel of God?"* Are we amazed that he could have been *"pure from the blood of all men"* without even *once* using the word hell? Could our bewilderment here be because we have been steeped in the traditions of men, and not in the traditions of Paul?

Therefore, brothers, stand fast, and hold the traditions which you have been taught, whether by word, or our epistle (II Thessalonians 2:15).

We are to hold Paul's traditions, *"whether by **word, or our epistle.***" Holding to Paul's very words and epistles will remove *hell* from our teaching.

*Hold fast the **form of sound words,** which you have **heard of me,** in faith and love which is in Christ Jesus* (II Timothy 1:13).

Again, *"holding fast the form of sound words"* that we have heard from Paul will remove *hell* from our doctrine.

We must be like those from Berea and search the Scriptures for ourselves (Acts 17:11). We need to test diligently, or prove the things that we believe against the Scriptures.

Prove all things; hold fast that which is good (I Thessalonians 5:21).

We need to see for ourselves if religious *hell* was a part of the vocabulary divinely given to Paul. We must consult an exhaustive concordance if need be. We must not settle for the party line, or a secondhand faith.

… Let every man be fully persuaded in his own mind (Romans 14:5).

Isn't Paul presented as our present pattern (I Timothy 1:15-16)?

Doesn't Paul tell us to follow him (I Corinthians 4:15-17; 11:1; Philippians 3:17)?

Didn't Paul tell us to,

*Hold fast the **form of sound words,** which you have **heard of me,** in faith and love which is in Christ Jesus* (II Timothy 1:13)?

Did we hear *hell* from Paul? Is it a Pauline form of *sound words?*

Have we been duped into accepting a religious tradition that is contrary to the sound scriptural teachings of our Apostle?

Wouldn't we be Pauline if we, like Paul, also excluded *hell* from our teaching?

Or, more pointedly, could we possibly be truly Pauline in our teaching, if we continue the use of a theological system that includes the traditional *hell?*

But speak the things which become **sound doctrine** (Titus 2:1).

The religious system's teaching concerning hell is *not* Pauline, and is *not* sound doctrine.

Let's not be afraid of where truth leads us. Truth truly liberates us from suppressive religious bondage. Well did our Savior say,

And you shall know the truth, and the truth shall make you free (John 8:32).

Why not enjoy the true freedom of believing the Scriptures over traditional teaching?

Why not follow Paul in a *pure* Grace Gospel that has *no* place for, nor need of a religious *hell?*

And the LORD God formed man of the dust of the ground, and breathed into his nostrils the breath of life; and man became a living soul.

~ Genesis 2:7

Chapter 4

LIFE AND DEATH

WHAT IS LIFE?

M an is the union of the dust of the ground (the body) and the breath of life (the spirit), creating a living soul. Thus, the two (the body and the spirit) joined together create a third (the soul). Body + spirit = soul.

This principle can be seen in the example of water (H_2O).

> The teaching of Scripture is (as we see it) that man consists of two parts: body and spirit; and that the union of these two makes a third thing, which is called "soul" or "living soul." Hence the word "soul" is used of the *whole personality; the living organism*.[1]

"Soul" Is Used as a Reference for Man

Young defines both the Hebrew word *nephes*" and the Greek word *psuche*, both translated as our English word *"soul,"* as "animal soul."[2] The idea being "animated, alive." That is why the word *"soul"* is used to speak of living man, as well as lower animal life (Numbers 31:28).

---

1. E.W. Bullinger, *The Rich Man and Lazarus*, Bible Student's Press™, Windber, PA, 2007, page 9.
2. Robert Young, *Analytical Concordance to the Bible*.

Strong also defines *nephesh* in the same way as Young, as "a breathing creature, *i.e.,* animal or vitality."[3] This definition matches the way that *"soul"* is used in Genesis 2.

And the LORD God formed man of the dust of the ground, and breathed into his nostrils the breath of life; and man became a living soul (Genesis 2:7).

When God breathed *"the breath of life,"* THEN man became a *"living soul"*; but when that *"breath of life"* leaves he will no longer be a *"soul"* (i.e., a breathing creature)!

The Hebrew word *nephesh* and the Greek word *psuche* have the exact same meaning, which can be seen by comparing Psalm 16:10 and Peter's quotation of it in Acts 2:27.

For You will not leave My soul [nephesh] in hell; neither will You suffer Your Holy One to see corruption (Psalm 16:10).

Because You will not leave My soul [psuche] in hell, neither will You suffer Your Holy One to see corruption" (Acts 2:27).

Here are a few simple examples from Scripture where we can see the usage of the word *"soul"* as a reference to living man.

*And Abram took Sarai his wife, and Lot his brother's son, and all their substance that they had gathered, and **the souls** that they had gotten in Haran; and they went forth to go into the land of Canaan; and into the land of Canaan they came (Genesis 12:5).*

In Genesis 36:6 the Hebrew word translated *"soul"* is also translated *"persons."*

*And Esau took his wives, and his sons, and his daughters, and all the **persons** [nephesh – souls] of his house, and his cattle, and all his beasts, and all his substance, which he had got in the land of Canaan; and went into the country from the face of his brother Jacob (Genesis 36:6).*

*These are the sons of Leah, which she bore unto Jacob in Padanaram, with his daughter Dinah: all **the souls** of his sons and his daughters were thirty*

---

3. James Strong, *The Exhaustive Concordance of the Bible*.

*and three. … All **the souls** that came with Jacob into Egypt, which came out of his loins, besides Jacob's sons' wives, all **the souls** were threescore and six* (Genesis 46:15, 26).

What Is Death?

Death is the opposite of life – it is the reversal of life. In death the spirit is removed from the body, and it is returned to God who gave it. Man is returned to the earth.

*Then shall the dust **return** to the earth as it was: and the spirit shall **return** unto God Who gave it* (Ecclesiastes 12:7).

*All go unto one place; all are of the dust, and all **turn** to dust again* (Ecclesiastes 3:20).

*In the sweat of your face shall you eat bread, until you **return** to the ground; for out of it were you taken: for dust you are, and unto dust shalt you **return*** (Genesis 3:19).

*His breath goes forth, he **returns** to his earth; in that very day his thoughts perish* (Psalm 146:4).

*… They die, and **return** to their dust* (Psalm 104:29).

Death is the absence of life, not life in some other form or place.

*… you shall die and **not live*** (II Kings 20:1).

*… The rest of the dead **lived not** again until …* (Revelation 20:4-6).

The Soul (Person) Will Die

Unlike what many believe and teach, the soul can and will die.

The soul who sins, shall die (Ezekiel 18:4).

… He spared not their soul from death, but gave their life over to the pestilence (Psalm 78:50).

Then He said to them, "My soul is exceeding sorrowful, even to death: tarry here, and watch with me" (Matthew 26:38).

And it shall come to pass, that every soul, who will not hear that prophet, shall be destroyed from among the people (Acts 3:23).

Satan's Great Lie

In the garden of Eden God told Adam,

you shall surely die (Genesis 2:17).

It was Satan's lie that,

*you shall **not** surely die* (Genesis 3:4).

E.W. Bullinger has written,

> So effectually has Satan's lie succeeded, and accomplished its purpose that, though the Lord Jesus said, *"I will come again and receive you unto myself,"* Christendom says, with one voice, "No! Lord. Thou needest not come for me: I will die and come to thee." Thus the blessed hope of resurrection and the coming of the Lord have been well nigh blotted out from the belief of the churches; and the promise of the Lord has been made of none effect by the ravages of tradition.[4]

Although death is sure for Adam and his descendants, so also is the hope of resurrection, as expressed by the Psalmist:

But God will redeem my soul from the power of the grave: for He shall receive me. Selah (Psalm 49:15).

---

4. Bullinger, page 16.

Who only has immortality, dwelling in the light which no man can approach unto; Whom no man has seen, nor can see: to Whom be honor and power everlasting. Amen.

~ I Timothy 6:16

Chapter 5

Is Man Immortal?

In the Scriptures, immortality is something that belongs intrinsically to God alone.

> *Now unto the King eternal, **immortal,** invisible, the only wise God, be honor and glory for ever and ever. Amen* (I Timothy 1:17).

> **Who only has immortality,** *dwelling in the light which no man can approach unto; Whom no man has seen, nor can see: to Whom be honor and power everlasting. Amen* (I Timothy 6:16).

Immortality is defined by Webster as "the quality of never ceasing to live or exist,"[1] and by Strong as "deathlessness."[2]

Resurrection brings immortality to man through the gospel of our Savior, the Lord Jesus Christ!

> *But is now made manifest by the appearing of our Savior Jesus Christ, Who has abolished death, and has brought life and immortality to light through the gospel* (II Timothy 1:10).

---

1. Noah Webster, *An American Dictionary of the English Language*, 1828.
2. James Strong, *The Exhaustive Concordance of the Bible*, Greek #110, *"Athanasia."*

Note that life and immortality are brought to light, *after* death has been abolished – Resurrection!

> *For this corruptible must put on incorruption, and this mortal must put on immortality* (I Corinthians 15:53).

When will man take on immortality?

The context of this chapter (I Corinthians 15) is clear: it will take place in *resurrection!* According to this verse, immortality is *not* something that man has, but something that must be *"put on."* In the resurrection God will clothe man in immortality!

Most of Christendom's theology teaches that man is already immortal. This is accomplished through the doctrine of the "immortality of the soul;" but as we have already seen, the soul is said to die. The teaching that man is immortal stands in contrast to the truth of Scripture and discounts the real need of resurrection. It is a pagan teaching espoused and made popular by Plato.

Luther on Immortality

> I permit the Pope to make articles of faith for himself and his faithful, such as … *the soul is immortal*, with all those monstrous opinions to be found in the Roman dung-hill of decretals.[3] (Martin Luther, in his response to Pope Leo X.)

Darby on Immortality

> We would express our conviction that the idea of *the immortality of the soul* has no source in the gospel; that it comes on the contrary from the Platonists and … the doctrine of *the immortality of the soul* came in to replace that of resurrection. This was about the time of Origen. … This view has taken the place of the doctrine of the resurrection of the church, as the epoch of its joy and glory.[4] (J.N. Darby, *The Hopes of the Church*, 1841.)

---

3. Cited by Otis Q. Sellers, *The Study of Human Destiny*, 1955, page 17.
4. Ibid.

The Effect of the False Teaching of Immortality on the Doctrine of Resurrection

The generally accepted view of death makes the grand experience of resurrection to be an anti-climax, and, of no essential value to the believer. If, as it is so confidently asserted, death ushers the believer into the presence of Christ, then resurrection can add nothing to this, neither can it accomplish anything that will in any way compare with its grand experience. If the "orthodox" conception of death is true, then the dead will be happy in heaven or miserable in hell whether they rise from the dead or not. But if scriptural conception is true, then resurrection is of the utmost importance, for without it then those who have fallen asleep in Christ have perished (I Corinthians 15:18).[5]

Since death is the result of the sin of one man (Adam), and resurrection is the result of the righteousness of one man (Christ), it cannot be right to make the result of Adam's sin to be the experience that will usher us into the blessings of Christ. We should be willing to reexamine any teaching that causes the hope of men in Christ to be in death rather than in resurrection. God's answer to death is resurrection. God's remedy for death is resurrection. We dishonor God's testimony when we make resurrection to be the reversal of a disembodied condition. Resurrection is the reversal of death.

We preach the death of Christ. But what would our answer be if an honest inquirer came to us asking if He really died, and if He were truly dead for three days and three nights. What answer would we give if asked, "If He had not risen from the dead, would He still be dead?" Would we still be able to say, "We do not preach a dead Christ," if He had not risen from the dead?

When the Apostle Paul sought to comfort the sorrowing saints in Thessalonica, did he comfort them by assuring them that their loved ones were happy in heaven, or did he set before them the hope of resurrection (I Thessalonians 4:13-18)? Did not the greatest Comforter Who ever spoke a word of consolation say to the one whose brother had recently died, *"Thy brother shall rise again"* (John 11:23)? If these questions are honestly considered they will increase the conviction that the whole matter of death and resurrection needs to be restudied.[6]

---

5. *And if Christ is not raised, your faith is vain; you are yet in your sins. Then they also who are fallen asleep in Christ are perished* (I Corinthians 15:17-18).
6. Sellers, pages 19-20.

> *For the wages of sin is death; but the gift of God is eternal life through*
> *Jesus Christ our Lord* (Romans 6:23).

I do not believe that the dead are either conscious or unconscious. These words can be applied only to the living. I believe that the dead are dead until the resurrection.[7]

Death being death, and not life, can be seen in Peter's description of the current condition of David.

> *Men and brothers, let me freely speak to you of the patriarch David, that he*
> *is both dead and buried, and his sepulcher is with us to this day … For David*
> *is not ascended into the heavens* (Acts 2:29, 34).

Conclusion

> *So when this corruptible shall have put on incorruption, and this mortal*
> *shall have put on immortality, then shall be brought to pass the saying that is*
> *written, Death is swallowed up in victory"* (I Corinthians 15:54).

Death is swallowed up in victory when Jesus Christ returns and raises the dead and transforms the living. … The teaching that man is inherently immortal robs Jesus Christ of glory that belongs to Him, for it is only through Him and His saving work that man receives immortality.[8]

---

7. Ibid., page 24.
8. Tom Ballinger, *Heaven Dwellers*.

And if Christ is not raised, your faith is vain; you are yet in your sins. Then they also who are fallen asleep in Christ are perished. If in this life only we have hope in Christ, we are of all men most miserable. But now is Christ risen from the dead, and become the firstfruits of them who slept. For since by man came death, by man came also the resurrection of the dead. For as in Adam all die, even so in Christ shall all be made alive. But every man in his own order: Christ the firstfruits; afterward they who are Christ's at His coming. Then comes the end, when He shall have delivered up the kingdom to God, even the Father; when He shall have put down all rule and all authority and power. For He must reign, until He has put all enemies under His feet. The last enemy that shall be destroyed is death.

~ I Corinthians 15:17-26

Chapter 6

THE HOPE OF RESURRECTION

THE HOPE OF THE AGES

Resurrection (not death) has always been the hope of God's people. This hope is based upon the promise of God:

I will ransom them from the power of the grave; I will redeem them from death: O death, I will be your plagues; O grave, I will be your destruction: repentance shall be hidden from my eyes (Hosea 13:14).

This hope is clearly expressed by Job:

For I know that my Redeemer lives, and that He shall stand at the latter day upon the earth: And though after my skin worms destroy this body, yet in my flesh shall I see God: Whom I shall see for myself, and my eyes shall behold, and not another; though my reins be consumed within me (Job 19:25-27).

Paul confirms that without the resurrection, there would be no hope:

And if Christ is not raised, your faith is vain; you are yet in your sins. Then they also who are fallen asleep in Christ are perished. If in this life only we have hope in Christ, we are of all men most miserable" (I Corinthians 15:17-19).

In fact, Paul devotes his longest chapter to this vital subject of resurrection (I Corinthians 15).

THE NEED FOR RESURRECTION

The reason that the truth of resurrection is so important is that man is appointed to death.

And as it is appointed unto men once to die ... (Hebrews 9:27).

For the wages of sin is death ... (Romans 6:23).

This appointment of death came upon man through Adam.

Wherefore, as by one man sin entered into the world, and death by sin; and so death passed upon all men, for that all have sinned (Romans 5:12).

For since by man came death, by man came also the resurrection of the dead. For as in Adam all die, even so in Christ shall all be made alive (I Corinthians 15:21-22).

THE CONDITION OF DEATH

Death is simple – it is the end of life. In the Scriptures the dead are dead, and are therefore always in contrast with the living.

In death there is no praise of the Lord.

Praise the LORD. Praise the LORD, O my soul. While I live will I praise the LORD: I will sing praises unto my God while I have any being (Psalm 146:1-2).

The dead praise not the LORD, neither any who go down into silence (Psalm 115:17).

In death man's breath leaves.

... His breath goeth forth ... (Psalm 146:4).

... You take away their breath, they die ... (Psalm 104:29).

In death man returns to the earth.

> *... He returns to his earth ...* (Psalm 146:4).

> *... They die, and return to their dust* (Psalm 104:29).

> *Then shall the dust return to the earth as it was ...* (Ecclesiastes 12:7).

In death man's thoughts perish.

> *... In that very day his thoughts perish* (Psalm 146:4).

In death man doesn't know anything.

> *For the living know that they shall die: but the dead know not anything ...* (Ecclesiastes 9:5).

> *Whatsoever your hand finds to do, do it with your might; for there is no work, nor device, nor knowledge, nor wisdom, in the grave, where you go* (Ecclesiastes 9:10).

In death man is silent.

> *The dead praise not the LORD, neither any who go down into silence* (Psalm 115:17).

GOD'S REMEDY FOR DEATH

God's remedy for death is so simple: it is the resurrection of the dead!

Man speaks of death as a friend, but God speaks of it as an enemy!

> *For He must reign, until He has put all enemies under His feet. The last enemy that shall be destroyed is death* (I Corinthians 15:25-26).

God will destroy death in resurrection!

> *But now is Christ risen from the dead, and become the firstfruits of them who slept. For since by man came death, by man came also the resurrection*

of the dead. For as in Adam all die, even so in Christ shall all be made alive. But every man in his own order: Christ the firstfruits; afterward they who are Christ's at His coming. Then comes the end, when He shall have delivered up the kingdom to God, even the Father; when He shall have put down all rule and all authority and power (I Corinthians 15:20-24).

DEATH LIKENED TO SLEEP

Death is likened unto sleep in the Scriptures.

"Lazarus sleeps" ... *Then said Jesus to them plainly, "Lazarus is dead"* (John 11:11, 14).

... Lest I sleep the sleep of death (Psalm 13:3).

... For now shall I sleep in the dust; and you shall seek me in the morning, but I shall not be (Job 7:21).

Why died I not ... for now should I have lain still and been quiet, I should have slept ... (Job 3:11-13).

... Them who sleep in the dust of the earth ... (Daniel 12:2).

And he kneeled down, and cried with a loud voice, "Lord, lay not this sin to their charge." And when he had said this, he fell asleep (Acts 7:60).

For David, after he had served his own generation by the will of God, fell on sleep, and was laid unto his fathers, and saw corruption (Acts 13:36).

... Them also who sleep in Jesus ... (I Thessalonians 4:14).

RESURRECTION LIKENED TO AWAKING

So, in contrast, resurrection is likened unto awaking from sleep in the Scriptures.

As for me, I will behold Your face in righteousness: I shall be satisfied, when I awake, with Your likeness (Psalm 17:15).

And many of them who sleep in the dust of the earth shall awake ... (Daniel 12:2).

ARE THE DEAD DEAD, OR ALIVE?

The Scriptures speak of the dead as not being alive.

But the rest of the dead lived not again until the thousand years were finished. This is the first resurrection (Revelation 20:5).

IS THERE LIFE AFTER DEATH?

Yes! In resurrection!

There is not life *in* death, but life *after* death! Christ's Own resurrection is our assurance of life *after* death.

And if Christ is not raised, your faith is vain; you are yet in your sins. Then they also who are fallen asleep in Christ are perished. If in this life only we have hope in Christ, we are of all men most miserable. But now is Christ risen from the dead, and become the firstfruits of them that slept. For since by man came death, by man came also the resurrection of the dead. For as in Adam all die, even so in Christ shall all be made alive. But every man in his own order: Christ the firstfruits; afterward they who are Christ's at His coming. Then comes the end, when He shall have delivered up the kingdom to God, even the Father; when He shall have put down all rule and all authority and power. For He must reign, until He has put all enemies under His feet. The last enemy that shall be destroyed is death (I Corinthians 15:17-26).

THAT BLESSED HOPE

Looking for that blessed hope, and the glorious appearing of the great God and our Savior Jesus Christ (Titus 2:13).

We have seen from the Scriptures that the hope of man has been the resurrection. To Paul, the apostle, God revealed a mystery in relation to resurrection. He called this mystery hope the *"blessed hope."* Some saints will bypass death and proceed straight to resurrection. This will be the blessed experience of those who are still alive at the coming of the Lord Jesus Christ.

I show you a mystery; We shall not all sleep, but we shall all be changed, in a moment, in the twinkling of an eye, at the last trump: for the trumpet shall sound, and the dead shall be raised incorruptible, and we shall be changed. For this corruptible must put on incorruption, and this mortal must put on immortality. So when this corruptible shall have put on incorruption, and this mortal shall have put on immortality, then shall be brought to pass the saying that is written, "Death is swallowed up in victory" (II Corinthians 15:51-54).

But I would not have you to be ignorant, brothers, concerning them who are asleep, that yoy sorrow not, even as others who have no hope. For if we believe that Jesus died and rose again, even so them also who sleep in Jesus will God bring with Him. For this we say unto you by the word of the Lord, that we who are alive and remain unto the coming of the Lord shall not prevent them who are asleep. For the Lord Himself shall descend from heaven with a shout, with the voice of the archangel, and with the trump of God: and the dead in Christ shall rise first: then we who are alive and remain shall be caught up together with them in the clouds, to meet the Lord in the air: and so shall we ever be with the Lord. Wherefore comfort one another with these words (I Thessalonians 4:13-18).

THE RESURRECTION AND THE GOSPEL

Many a gospel message has been spoiled and robbed of its power by omitting the great truth of the resurrection.[1]

Who was delivered for our offences, and was raised again for our justification (Romans 4:25).

For I delivered to you first of all that which I also received, how that Christ died for our sins according to the Scriptures; and that He was buried, and that He rose again the third day according to the Scriptures (I Corinthians 15:3-4).

Failure to grasp the truth concerning death strikes at the very heart of the gospel. Whatever the wages of sin is, Jesus Christ endured it to the full, in order to become man's Saviour. If the wages of sin is eternal punishment,

---

1. Stuart Allen, *Resurrection and the Purpose of the Ages*, Berean Publishing Trust, 1957.

Jesus Christ could not be the Saviour of anyone, for He did not endure that. *"The wages of sin is death"* (Romans 6:23). *"Christ died for our sins, was buried and was raised the third day"* (I Corinthians 15:1-5).[2]

Resurrection is at the very heart of the gospel.

2. Tom Ballanger, *Heaven Dwellers.*

But now he is dead, wherefore should I fast? Can I bring him back again? I shall go to him, but he shall not return to me.

~ II Samuel 12:23

Chapter 7

WHERE DO BABIES GO WHEN THEY DIE?

Here is the age-old question: "Where do babies go when they die?" Even though the topic is sometimes hotly debated, the answer is really quite simple.

They go where everyone goes when they die – to the grave.

For that which befalls the sons of men befalls beasts; even one thing befalls them: as the one dies, so dies the other; yes, they have all one breath; so that a man has no preeminence above a beast: for all is vanity. All go unto one place; all are of the dust, and all turn to dust again (Ecclesiastes 3:19-20).

David had an infant son who died, to which he responded,

*But now he is dead, wherefore should I fast? can I bring him back again? **I shall go to him,** but he shall not return to me (II Samuel 12:23).*

David fully expected to join his son one day.

So the issue is simple: if we know where David went when he died, we would know where his son went. Just where did David go when he died? What does the Bible actually tell us?

David went where everyone goes when they die:

> So David **slept with his fathers, and was buried** … (I Kings 2:10).

David is not in heaven, or in a fiery hell, or in paradise. David is buried and in the grave. Peter attested to this clear truth:

> Men and brothers, let me freely speak to you of the patriarch David, that **he is both dead and buried,** and his sepulcher is with us to this day (Acts 2:29).

> **For David is not ascended into the heavens** … (Acts 2:34).

Paul also confirmed the truth of David's whereabouts.

> For David, after he had served his own generation by the will of God, **fell on sleep, and was laid unto his fathers, and saw corruption** (Acts 13:36).

David and his son, along with all the dead, are in the grave awaiting resurrection:

> … All who are in their graves shall hear His voice (John 5:28).

> … Them who sleep in the dust shall awake … (Daniel 12:2).

> I will ransom them from the power of the grave; I will redeem them from death … (Hosea 13:14).

> And if Christ is not raised, your faith is vain; you are yet in your sins. Then they also who are fallen asleep in Christ are perished. If in this life only we have hope in Christ, we are of all men most miserable (I Corinthians 15:17-19).

And when he had consulted with the people, he appointed singers to the LORD, and that should praise the beauty of holiness, as they went out before the army, and to say, "Praise the LORD; for His mercy endures for ever."

~ II Chronicles 20:21

Chapter 8

THE BEAUTY OF HOLINESS

GOD'S TRUE CHARACTER REVEALED

Christendom misrepresents God to mankind as a harsh, stern, angry god, full of wrath. This is the byproduct of the religious system's faulty estimation of God's holiness. We have been seriously misled as to the true nature of our Creator.

When the choir of Israel sang the praises of God, it is quite interesting to note what they specifically magnified about Him:

> ... *He appointed singers unto the LORD, and that they should* **praise the beauty of holiness** ... (II Chronicles 20:21).

To demonstrate *the beauty of His holiness*, here is what they actually sang:

> ... *Praise the LORD;* **for His mercy endures for ever** (II Chronicles 20:21).

The religious system would lead us to believe that the holiness of God overflows with sternest severity, anger, and wrath; but when the choir of Israel sang the praises of God's holiness, they specifically sang about His mercy enduring for ever. This is contrary to religious thinking.

The holiness of God actually overflows with kindness, compassion, love, gentleness, and mercy! We learn this from the pages of the Scriptures themselves. We see this clearly within the context of our passage. God's holiness is associated with divine mercy.

Let's look at a few other passages, where we can clearly see the relationship between God's holiness and His mercy.

> For thus says the high and lofty One Who inhabits eternity, **Whose name is Holy** ... "I will not contend forever, neither will I be always wroth ..." (Isaiah 57:15-16).

> I will not execute the fierceness of mine anger, I will not return to destroy Ephraim: **for** I am God, and not man; **the Holy One** in the midst of you ... (Hosea 11:9).

Why would God not execute the fierceness of His anger? The verse tells us why: because He is not man, He is "the Holy One!"

We can also see the connection between the holiness of God and His mercy in the earthly life of the Lord Jesus Christ. The one "Who is holy" and "separate from sinners" was here on earth as "a friend of Publicans and sinners" (c.f. Hebrews 7:26; Matthew 11:19).

One telling passage about the true nature of holiness can be seen in the admonition of Paul, the apostle:

> I will therefore that men pray everywhere, lifting up **holy hands, without wrath** and doubting (I Timothy 2:8).

Ultimately, wrath and holiness are not compatible in the mind of Paul (nor the mind of God!).

Here is another passage that sheds great light on the true character of holiness:

> Brothers, if a man is overtaken in a fault, you who are spiritual, restore such an one in the **spirit of meekness** ... (Galatians 6:1).

Genuine spirituality and true holiness produce gentleness, kindness, love, compassion, and mercy. The absence of these characteristics is a result of the lack of the holiness of God appropriated to the life of the believer. It is the false holiness of self-righteousness that produces the arrogance and conceit of haughtiness (*i.e.,* a "better-than-thou" attitude).

> *The servant of the Lord must not strive; but be **gentle unto all men,** apt to teach, patient, in meekness instructing those who oppose themselves ...* (II Timothy 2:24-25).

In closing, we will recall that God's holiness is predominantly connected with His Saviorhood! He is the compassionate and loving Savior *because* of His holiness ... not in spite of it!

> *For I am the LORD your God, the Holy One of Israel, your Savior ..."* (Isaiah 43:3).

This is the biblical view of the true and living God!

Rejoice in Him! He is a wonderful God! His holiness is beautiful!

This is a faithful saying, and worthy of all acceptation, that Christ Jesus came into the world to save sinners; of whom I am chief. Howbeit for this cause I obtained mercy, that in me first Jesus Christ might show forth all longsuffering, for a pattern to them who should hereafter believe on Him to life everlasting. Now unto the King eternal, immortal, invisible, the only wise God, be honor and glory for ever and ever. Amen.

~ I Timothy 1:15-17

Chapter 9

PAUL: THE PATTERN OF SALVATION FOR THE UNBELIEVER

Many believers know and understand that Paul is the apostle for this current dispensation, and that he is the source for the knowledge of God's will, His plan and purpose for us today. It is often heard that "Paul is our pattern," and therefore one must experience their salvation in a similar manner as Paul. Yet, is Paul really the *"pattern"* for *our* salvation today? Is this really what I Timothy 1:15-17 is saying?

PAUL'S CONVERSION

Paul was saved in a very different way than we are. His was a salvation by direct divine intervention. Listen in part to Paul give an account of his conversion.

And it came to pass, that, as I made my journey, and came near to Damascus about noon, suddenly there shined from heaven a great light round about me. And I fell unto the ground, and heard a voice saying to me, "Saul, Saul, why are you persecuting Me?" And I answered, "Who are You, Lord? And He said to me, "I am Jesus of Nazareth, Whom you are persecuting." And they who were with me saw indeed the light, and were afraid; but they heard not the voice of Him Who spoke to me ... And when I could not see for the glory of that light, being led by the hand of them who were with me, I came into Damascus (Acts 22:6-11).

Damascus Road Experience

Saul did not believe by simple faith (apart from sight). It took the "Damascus Road experience" to bring him to Christ. He met up with the resurrected Christ! Oh, the extent to which God will go to reach man! He is much less limited than we are in His evangelism.

Paul the Pattern of Things to Come

Paul says that his salvation is a pattern for those who should believe *"hereafter,"* and this salvation shows forth all of God's *"longsuffering."*

Paul is not only our Apostle in this current age of the Dispensation of the Grace of God, but he is God's pattern, or type of the salvation of unbelievers *after their death* (hereafter). The unbelieving, the obstinate, the oppressors, the enemies of God will all have a dramatic conversion, coming face-to-face with their Savior in the resurrection.

OUR CONVERSION

Considering the above, then, are we saved as Paul was saved? Hardly: Saul, who later was called Paul, was an archenemy of God. It took the direct hand of God to stop him in his tracks and turn him around.

When Paul wrote to Timothy he said that his salvation was *"a pattern"* (i.e., a type, a picture); but it was not a pattern of *our* salvation. Our conversion in no way resembles his.

Blessed Are They Who Have Not Seen, and Yet Have Believed

For those of us who have the privilege of believing now, we are indeed greatly blessed. We are taught this from another account in the Scriptures. It is in the record of "doubting Thomas." Listen to what Thomas, the apostle said.

> *The other disciples therefore said to him* [Thomas], *"We have seen the Lord." But he said to them, "Except I shall see in His hands the print of the nails, and put my finger into the print of the nails, and thrust my hand into His side, I will not believe"* (John 20:25).

Now listen to the response of our Lord Jesus Christ to Thomas.

> *Then He said to Thomas, "Reach your finger here, and behold My hands; and reach your hand hither, and thrust it into My side: and be not faithless, but believing." And Thomas answered and said to Him, "My Lord and my God." Jesus said to him, "Thomas, because you have seen Me, you have believed: blessed are they who have not seen, and yet have believed"* (John 20:27-29).

Jesus said that Thomas believed by sight – *"Because you have seen Me, you have believed."* He goes on to say, *"blessed are they who have not seen, and yet have believed."*

The First Trusters

Those of us today who believe by simple faith (apart from sight) are but the first trusters.

> *That **we** should be to the praise of His glory, **who first trusted** in Christ* (Ephesians 1:12).

Do not be discouraged as you look around you. What you see is not the end of God's plan and purpose. Granted, the world is filled with sin and unbelief; but God is not yet done. Don't judge the final outcome by the current state of things. This is not the finished product of God.

Those of us who now trust the Lord Jesus Christ are but the beginning of God's glorious work. We are but the first trusters in His glorious design.

The Firstfruits of the Harvest

> *… My wellbeloved Epaenetus, who is **the firstfruits** of Achaia unto Christ* (Romans 16:5).

> *Of His Own will He begot us with the Word of Truth, that we should be **a kind of firstfruits of His creatures*** (James 1:18).

> *… These were redeemed from among men, being **the firstfruits unto God** and to the Lamb* (Revelation 14:4).

In every harvest there is that small portion of the crop that matures early, before the vast majority of the rest. The firstfruits are a token of that which is to come – the full harvest.

Under the Old Testament economy the firstfruits belonged to God, and were holy unto Him.

In every generation and in every place, God has had His firstfruits; those that come to harvest earlier than the rest. We are blessed of God to be the firstfruits of God's full harvest. We will enjoy the First Resurrection; but this does not exclude the rest of creation, who are awaiting our manifestation:

> *For the earnest expectation of the creature waits for the manifestation of the sons of God* Romans 8:19).

What a blessed privilege to be the first trusters – the firstfruits of the Lord. Just as God has brought us to faith, He also will bring the rest of His creation.

"HEREAFTER" CONVERSIONS

Not Saved After Paul's Pattern

None of us in the Dispensation of Grace were saved after the pattern of Paul; but *"them who should hereafter believe on Him"* will see *"a light from heaven, above the brightness of the sun."* They will come into the presence of the resurrected Son of God and will with Saul call Him Lord.

> *That at the name of Jesus every knee should bow, of things in heaven, and things in earth, and things under the earth; And that **every tongue should confess** that Jesus Christ is Lord, to the glory of God the Father* (Philippians 2:10).

This confession that Jesus Christ is Lord can only be the work of the Holy Spirit!

> *… No man can say that Jesus is the Lord, but by the Holy Spirit* (I Corinthians 12:3).

A closer look at what Paul actually said will reveal that he did not tell Timothy that his salvation was a pattern for ours. He says that his conversion was a pattern not for now, but for *"them which should **hereafter** believe."*

Hereafter

A definition of *"hereafter"* found in the Webster's Dictionary is "in a future state" (*American Dictionary of the English Language*, 1828).

The Greek word is *Strong's Greek Lexicon #3195, mello*. Here are some examples of how this *same* Greek word was translated elsewhere in the *King James Version*.

*... Who has warned you to flee from the wrath **to come** [mello]?* (Matthew 3:7).

*... Neither in this world, neither in the world **to come** [mello]* (Matthew 12:32).

*... Who has warned you to flee from the wrath **to come** [mello]?* (Luke 3:7).

*... Nor things **to come** [mello]* (Romans 8:38).

*... Or things present, or things **to come** [mello]* (I Corinthians 3:22).

*... Not only in this world, but also in that which is **to come** [mello]* (Ephesians 1:21).

*Which are a shadow of things **to come** [mello] ...* (Colossians 2:17).

*... Having promise of the life that now is, and of that which is **to come** [mello]* (I Timothy 4:8).

*For unto the angels has He not put in subjection the world **to come** [mello] ...* (Hebrews 2:5).

*And have tasted the good Word of God, and the powers of the world **to come** [mello]* (Hebrews 6:5).

*But Christ being come a high priest of good things **to come** [mello] ...* (Hebrews 9:11).

*For the law having a shadow of good things **to come** [mello] ...* (Hebrews 10:1).

> For here have we no continuing city, but we seek one **to come** [mello] (Hebrews 13:14).

Clearly the Greek word *mello* speaks of that which is *"to come,"* and the word *"hereafter"* in I Timothy 1:16 speaks of the *"hereafter."*

The Victorious God

How have we made death the end of God's grace and mercy?

Reflecting upon the two examples of Thomas and Paul, we come to realize that God has, and will directly and miraculously intervene in the faith of some individuals, by giving them sight experience for their faith. God will not deny this experience to the precious multitudes of His creation. Christendom has missed a key ingredient in the understanding of God, His love, and His will.

Like Saul, the real question is not really one of unbelief, but simply one of *timing.* All will eventually be brought to belief by their Creator, although not all in their lifetime. Some will be saved by pure *"faith"* without sight, while with others it will take *"sight"* to believe.

It is God's will that *all* men be saved (I Timothy 2:4). God does *all things* after the counsel of His Own will (Ephesians 1:11). His love will never fail (I Corinthians 13:8). He will not lose any of His creatures. He will be victorious in all for all eternity. He will be *"All in all."* Just as God subdued Saul on the Damascus road, He shall subdue *all things* unto Himself.

> And when all things shall be subdued unto Him, then shall the Son also Himself be subject unto Him Who put all things under Him, that God may be **All in all** (I Corinthians 15:28).

Then his master shall bring him to the judges; he shall also bring him to the door, or to the door post; and his master shall bore his ear through with an aul; and he shall serve him forever.

~ Exodus 21:6

Chapter 10

FOREVER, ETERNAL AND EVERLASTING

S ometimes we are confident that we know the meaning of words and terms. Their definitions seem so fixed and settled in our minds. For instance, what does *"for ever"* actually mean? Are we sure we know? Just how long is *"forever?"*

At our first look into the subject, *"forever"* would surely seem to be something about which we could be absolute; but as we look closely at the Scriptures, we will be amazed to find that our definition is not biblical.

Words are simply vehicles to communicate ideas of understanding. As one author clearly has written,

> In all languages, it is usage that determines meaning … Since usage always determines meaning, biblical usage, certainly, always determines biblical meaning.[1]

Actual scriptural usage of *"forever"* will clearly demonstrate it cannot carry the religious meaning of "unending" that we have been brought up to accept. Let's look at a few examples of the usage of *"forever,"* where the scriptural meaning obviously cannot mean "without end."

---

1. Loyal Hurley, *The Outcome of Infinite Grace*, Bible Student's Press™.

Jonah and the Whale

The first passage we shall look at is a reference to how long Jonah was in the belly of the whale.

> *I went down to the bottoms of the mountains; the earth with her bars was about me **forever**: yet You have brought up my life from corruption, O LORD my God* (Jonah 2:6).

Jonah uses the word *"forever"* in reference to his ordeal, but he clearly defines its length as only three days and three nights:

> *Now the LORD had prepared a great fish to swallow up Jonah. And Jonah was in the belly of the fish **three days and three nights*** (Jonah 1:17).

The Lord Jesus confirmed this duration.

> *For as Jonas was **three days and three nights** in the whale's belly; so shall the Son of man be three days and three nights in the heart of the earth* (Matthew 12:40).

The usage of *"forever"* in Jonah 2:6 simply cannot carry the meaning of "unending."

The Servant

The next passage we shall consider is in reference to how long a willing servant would be indentured to his master.

> *Then his master shall bring him to the judges; he shall also bring him to the door, or to the door post; and his master shall bore his ear through with an aul; and he shall serve him **forever*** (Exodus 21:6).

Here, *"forever"* could not possibly have extended past the servant's lifespan. The usage of *"forever"* in Exodus 21:6 simply cannot carry the sense of "unending."

Solomon's Temple

Another example we see of the scriptural usage of *"forever"* is related to Solomon's

Temple. After it was dedicated, the Lord said He would put His name there *"forever."*

> And the LORD said to him, *"I have heard your prayer and your supplication, that you have made before me: I have hallowed this house, which you have built, to put My name there **forever*** (I Kings 9:3).

Interestingly, Solomon's Temple stood for a period of only about 400 years. Thus, the usage of *"forever"* in I Kings 9:3 simply cannot carry the definition of "unending" either.

Ten Generations

In the following passage, *"forever"* is clearly defined as ten generations:

> An Ammonite or Moabite shall not enter into the congregation of the LORD; **even to their tenth generation** shall they not enter into the congregation of the LORD **forever** (Deuteronomy 23:3).

The usage of *"forever"* here in Deuteronomy 23:3 simply cannot carry the definition of "unending" either, since it has been set by the context for a period of ten generations.

"Forever ... Until"

The last example we shall consider in this brief study is found in the book of Isaiah.

> ... The forts and towers shall be for dens **forever ... until** the Spirit is poured upon us from on high, and the wilderness be a fruitful field, and the fruitful field be counted for a forest (Isaiah 32:14-15).

In this prophecy, this *"forever"* condition would remain *"until"* a time when the Spirit would be poured out. Thus again, the usage of *"forever"* here, as in the other passages we have considered, simply cannot carry the meaning of "unending."

Loyal Hurley has noted the significance of *"forever"* in the first three passages:

Here is something that ought to be clear to any intelligent, honest man. A word that is used to mean, in one case, three days and nights, in another case, a man's lifetime, and in still another, a period of about four centuries, surely does not mean unending or eternal – no matter what English word is used to translate it. Usage determines meaning.[2]

THE "FOREVER" FAMILY OF WORDS

The principle here does not just apply to *"forever,"* but to an entire family of English words used in Bible translation. Our English words *"eternal"* and *"everlasting"* are among those in this family. These words also often carry with them the religious idea of "endless."

"Eternal" and *"everlasting"* are but alternate words used to translate the Hebrew or Greek words that have also been translated *"forever."* So just as *"forever"* does not carry the idea of *"endlessness,"* neither do *"eternal"* or *"everlasting."*

The Hebrew Word

The Old Testament Hebrew word used to translate *"forever"* is ʽôlâm *(o-lawm´)*. It is also translated in the *King James Version* by the following English words:

>   *any time* (Leviticus 25:32).
>   *of old* (Deuteronomy 32:7).
>   *old time* (Joshua 24:2).
>   *ancient times* (Psalms 77:5).
>   *long* (Ecclesiastes 12:5).

The Greek Word

The Greek word *aiōn* (aion, "ahee-ohn´") (and its forms) is the word used to translate *"forever," "eternal"* and *"everlasting."* This word does not have as its meaning "endless duration" as our religious traditions have taught us; rather it denotes a limited duration, an interval of time. Thus, it is also used to translate our English words *"ages,"* or *"world."*

The Greek noun *aiōn* is used 128 times. It is translated in the *King James Version* as follows:

---

2. *Ibid.*, Hurley.

Ages	2	Evermore	4
Course	1	Never	7
Eternal	2	World	40
Ever	72		

The Greek adjective *aiōnios* ("ahee-o'-nee-os") is used 71 times. It is translated in the *King James Version* as follows:

Eternal	42	Everlasting	4
Ever	1	World	40

ETYMOLOGY, DEFINITION AND USAGE

Now, let's take a closer look at this Greek word *aiōn*. We will look at its etymology, definition, and usage.

Etymology

Etymology gives no warrant for applying the idea of eternity to the word … We find no reason in its etymology for giving it the sense of endless duration. – J.W. Hanson, *The Greek Word Aion*, 1875 (pages 10, 11).

It must be admitted that the Greek word which is rendered *"eternal"* does not, in itself, involve endlessness, but rather, duration, whether through an age or succession of ages, and that it is therefore applied in the New Testament to periods of time that have had both a beginning and ending. – Charles John Ellicott, *Ellicott's Commentary on the Whole Bible*.

Definition

The time of life. – Hesychius (A.D. 400-600).

An interval denoting time. – Theodoret (A.D. 300-400).

Properly, an age. – James Strong, *Strong's Exhaustive Concordance, Greek Lexicon* (Greek #165).

Primarily signifies time, in the sense of age, or generation. – *International Standard Bible Encyclopedia* (page 1010).

An age. – W.E. Vine, *Vine's Expository Dictionary.*

A period of time related to the subject. – Charles J. Wilhelm, *Biblical Dyslexia* (2004), Page 80.

Any space of time whether longer or shorter, past, present or future, to be determined by the persons or things spoken of, and the scope of the subjects; the life or age of man. Aionios, a definite and long period of time, that is, a long enduring, but still definite period of time. – John Schleusner, *Novus Thesaurus Philologico-Criticus* (1829).

The life that hastes away in the breathing of our breath, life as transitory; then the course of life, time of life, and general life in its temporal form, then, the space of human life, an age. – E.W. Bullinger, *A Critical Lexicon and Concordance.*

A period of existence; one's lifetime; life; an age; a generation; a long space of time. A space of time clearly defined and marked out; an era, epoch, age, period or dispensation. – Liddell and Scott's *Greek-English Lexicon.*

Time; space of time; life time and life; the ordinary period of man's life; the age of man; man's estate; a long period of time. – James Donnegan, *A New Greek and English Lexicon* (1839).

Aion: A space of time, as a lifetime, generation, period of history, an indefinitely long period. – Abbott-Smith, *Manual Greek Lexicon of the New Testament.*

Our Everyday Usage of the Word "Forever"

It is indeed interesting to see the wide range of time periods that *"forever"* can cover. It all depends upon the usage of the word – the context in which it is set. Is this not exactly the way we use *"forever"* in our own daily speech? For example, we might hear someone say,

"I could not believe how many people were at the grocery store. I was in the checkout line forever."

"I will be thirty next month, and I still have not found a mate. I have been looking for a wife forever."

"I'll be able to retire in two years. It won't come quick enough for me, I have been working here in this factory forever."

"This bedroom suite has been in our family forever."

In none of these examples do we convey the meaning of time as being "without end." In fact, in each of these examples, we may determine by the context of usage an estimate of the duration of time.

In the first example, we may expect that someone could spend 10 to 20 minutes or so in line. That might be the context of the usage of "forever."

In the second example, one might expect that the young man has been seeking a wife for ten years or so.

In the next example, we might expect that the soon-to-be retiree has worked at the factory for twenty, thirty, or forty years.

Then in our last example, one might expect that forever could refer to a number of generations, maybe even a hundred or two hundred years.

In other words, in each case the usage of "forever" in its context would determine its meaning. We would not expect someone to stand in a checkout line for twenty, thirty, or forty years. Neither would we expect the bedroom suite to have been in the family for 10 to 20 minutes.

Yet by our own daily usage of the word "forever," we could mean any one of these expansive ranges of meanings. Usage and context always determine meaning.

"Forever" does not carry a scriptural meaning of "without end." The only time *"forever"* means "without end" is when it comes to religious language.

Scriptural Usage

In this section we shall see verses where the Greek words *aiōn* and *aiōnios* are translated. We have selected verses that clearly demonstrate that these Greek words cannot possibly mean "endless" or "unending."

*He also who received seed among the thorns is he who hears the Word;
and the care of this **world** [aiōn], and the deceitfulness of riches, choke the
word, and he becomes unfruitful (Matthew 13:22).*

*The enemy who sowed them is the devil; the harvest is the end of the **world**
[aiōn]; and the reapers are the angels (Matthew 13:39).*

*As He spoke by the mouth of His holy prophets, who have been since the
world [aiōn] began (Luke 1:70).*

*And the lord commended the unjust steward, because he had done wisely:
for the children of this **world** [aiōn] are in their generation wiser than the
children of light (Luke 16:8).*

*Since the **world** [aiōn] began was it not heard that any man opened the
eyes of one who was born blind (John 9:32).*

*Now to Him Who is of power to establish you according to my gospel, and
the preaching of Jesus Christ, according to the revelation of the mystery,
which was kept secret since the **world** [aiōnios] began (Romans 16:25).*

*Wherefore, if meat makes my brother to offend, I will eat no flesh while the
world [aiōn] stands, lest I make my brother to offend (I Corinthians 8:13).*

*Now all these things happened to them for examples: and they are written
for our admonition, upon whom the ends of the **world** [aiōn] are come (I
Corinthians 10:11).*

*That in the **ages** [aiōn] to come He might show the exceeding riches of His
grace in His kindness toward us through Christ Jesus (Ephesians 2:7).*

*Even the mystery which has been hidden from **ages** [aiōn] and from generations, but now is made manifest to His saints (Colossians 1:26).*

*Charge them who are rich in this **world** [aiōn], that they be not highminded,
nor trust in uncertain riches, but in the living God, Who gives us richly all
things to enjoy (I Timothy 6:17).*

Who has saved us, and called us with a holy calling, not according to our *works, but according to His Own purpose and grace, which was given us in Christ Jesus before the **world** [aiōnion] began* (II Timothy 1:9).

*In hope of eternal life, which God, Who cannot lie, promised before the **world** [aiōnion] began* (Titus 1:2).

*But unto the Son He said, "Your throne, O God, is **for ever** [aiōn] and **ever** [aion]: a scepter of righteousness is the scepter of Your kingdom"* (Hebrews 1:8).

*For then must He often have suffered since the foundation of the world: but now once in the end of the **world** [aiōn] has He appeared to put away sin by the sacrifice of Himself* (Hebrews 9:26).

Sodom and Gomorrha are said to be suffering the vengeance of **eternal** [aionios] fire:

*Even as Sodom and Gomorrha, and the cities about them in like manner, giving themselves over to fornication, and going after strange flesh, are set forth for an example, suffering the vengeance of **eternal** [aiōnios] fire* (Jude 1:7).

Yet we know this *"eternal fire"* is not endless, because God has promised their own future restoration at the time when He restores Israel!

*When your sisters, **Sodom and her daughters, shall return to their former estate,** and Samaria and her daughters shall return to their former estate, then you and your daughters shall return to your former estate* (Ezekiel 16:55).

THE RELIGIOUS CONCEPT OF "ETERNAL"

Interestingly enough, our English word *"eternal"* comes from the Latin *æternus* which means, literally, "lasting for an age." – Walter Skeat, *The Concise Dictionary of English Etymology*, 1882. This is confirmed by many etymological sources:

"lasting for an age" – John Kennedy, *Word Stems: A Dictionary*, 1996 (page 128).

"age" – Robert K. Barnhart, *Barnhart's Concise Dictionary of Etymology,*
1995 (page 254).

"age" – Ernest Weekly, *An Etymological Dictionary of Modern English,* 1967
(page 526).

Somewhere along the way the meaning of the word "eternal" took on its modern
religious concept. "Eternal" has come to mean "endless." This definition is purely
religious, rooted in Greek philosophy.

The Testimony of Others

We are not alone in coming to see the important scriptural meaning of *"forever,"*
"eternal," and *"everlasting."* Consider the testimony of others concerning the
current concept of "endless" as related to "eternity:"

> No, doubt it was right at one time to translate *aion* by eternal, and would
> be right again could we reinstate the original significance of the word: for,
> strangely enough, the word "eternal" originally meant age-long. – Samuel
> Cox, *Salvator Mundi, or Is Christ the Saviour of All Men?* 1877 (Page 119).

> Let me say to Bible students that we must be very careful how we use the
> word "eternity." We have fallen into great error in our constant use of that
> word. There is no word in the whole Book of God corresponding with our
> "eternal" which as commonly used among us means absolutely without end.
> – G. Campbell Morgan, *God's Methods With Men* (page 185).

> Eternity is not a Biblical theme … What we have to learn is that the Bible does
> not speak of eternity. It is not written to tell us of eternity. Such a consideration
> is entirely outside the scope of revelation. – Charles H. Welch, *An Alphabetical
> Analysis* (Vol. 1, p. 279, 52).

> *"Aion"* … is a period of longer or shorter duration, having a beginning and
> an end, and complete in itself … The word always carries the notion of time,
> and not of eternity. It always means a period of time. Otherwise it would be
> impossible to account for the plural, or for such qualifying expressions as this
> age, or the age to come. It does not mean something endless or everlasting
> … The adjective *"aionios"* in like manner carries the idea of time. Neither the
> noun nor the adjective, in themselves, carry the sense of endless or everlasting

... Words which are habitually applied to things temporal or material cannot carry in themselves the sense of endlessness. Even when applied to God, we are not forced to render *"aionios"* everlasting. Of course the life of God is endless; but the question is whether, in describing God as *"aionios,"* it was intended to describe the duration of his being, or whether some different and larger idea was not contemplated. – Marvin Vincent, *Word Studies in the New Testament* (Vol. IV, p. 59).

That *"aiónion"* does not mean endless or eternal, may appear from considering that no adjective can have a greater force than the noun from which it is derived. If *"aión"* means age (which none either will or can deny) then *"aiónion"* must mean age-lasting, or duration through the age or ages to which the thing spoken of relates. – Nathaniel Scarlett (1798).

Since *aion* meant "age," *"aionios"* means, properly, "belonging to an age," or "age-long," and anyone who asserts that it must mean "endless" defends a position which even Augustine practically abandoned twelve centuries ago. – Frederic William Farrar, *Mercy and Judgment,* (page 378).

The Bible hardly speaks of eternity in a philosophical sense of infinite duration without beginning or end. The Hebrew word *"olam"* ... in contexts where it is traditionally translated *"forever,"* means, in itself, no more than "for an indefinitely long period." ... In the New Testament, *"aion"* is used as the equivalent of *"olam."* – *Encyclopedic Dictionary of the Bible.*

The Old Testament and the New Testament are not acquainted with the conception of eternity as timelessness. The Old Testament has not developed a special term for *"eternity."* The word *aion* originally meant "vital force," "life;" then "age," "lifetime." It is, however, also used generally of a (limited or unlimited) long space of time ... – *The Interpreter's Dictionary of the Bible* (Vol. IV, p. 643).

There is no word either in the Old Testament Hebrew or in the New Testament Greek to express the abstract idea of eternity. (Vol. III, p. 369): Eternal, everlasting-nonetheless *"eternal"* is misleading, inasmuch as it has come in the English to connote the idea of "endlessly existing," and thus to be practically a synonym for *"everlasting."* But this is not an adequate rendering of *"aionios"* which varies in meaning with the variations of the noun *"aion"* from which it comes. – *Hasting's Dictionary of the New Testament* (p. 370).

The word by itself, whether adjective or substantive, never means endless.
– Frederic William Farrar, *The Wider Hope* (1890).

The conception of eternity, in the Semitic languages, is that of a long duration and series of ages. – J.S. Blunt, *Dictionary of Theology.*

The word *"aion"* is never used in Scripture, or anywhere else, in the sense of endlessness (vulgarly called eternity, it always meant, both in Scripture and out, a period of time); else how could it have a plural -- how could you talk of the æons and æons of æons as the Scripture does? – Charles Kingsley (1857), *Endless Torments Unscriptural.*

"Aion" means "an age," a limited period, whether long or short, though often of indefinite length; and the adjective *"aionios"* means "of the age," "age-long," "aeonian," and never "everlasting" (of its own proper force). It is true that it may be applied as an epithet to things that are endless, but the idea of endlessness in all such cases comes not from the epithet, but only because it is inherent in the object to which the epithet is applied, as in the case of God. – Thomas Allin, *Christ Triumphant.*

Age

The single most commonly used English word that represents the meaning of *aiōn* is *"age."* Twice the *King James Version* translators used the word *"ages"* to translate *aiōn* (Ephesians 2:7; Colossians 1:26).

*That in the **ages** [aiōn] to come He might show the exceeding riches of His grace in His kindness toward us through Christ Jesus (Ephesians 2:7).*

*Even the mystery which has been hidden from **ages** [aiōn] and from generations, but now is made manifest to His saints (Colossians 1:26).*

Etymologically, the words *"age"* and *"eternal"* are from the same source. This can be verified by checking any dictionary on word origins. As an example, Eric Partridge in his work, *Origins: A Short Etymological Dictionary of Modern English* (1983) has the following listed under "Eternal" – "See Age."

Our English word *"age"* best represents the concept of the word *aiōn* in the Divine plan. When God uses *aiōn* in reference to His workings, He communicates the idea of *"age"* (or *"eon"*). Or, in the case of *aiōnios* it would be *"age-lasting,"* but once again the *"age"* in reference must be qualified by usage within the context.

WHAT THE SCRIPTURES ACTUALLY TEACH US
ABOUT THE AGES (*aiōns*) OF GOD

The Ages (*aiōns*) Have a Beginning.

*Has in these last days spoken unto us by His Son, Whom He has appointed heir of all things, by Whom also He made the **worlds** [aion] (Hebrews 1:2).*

*But we speak the wisdom of God in a mystery, even the hidden wisdom, which God ordained before the **world** [aiōn] unto our glory (I Corinthians 2:7).*

*Who has saved us, and called us with a holy calling, not according to our works, but according to His Own purpose and grace, which was given us in Christ Jesus before the **world** [aionios] began (II Timothy 1:9).*

The Ages (*aiōns*) Have an End, Individually and Collectively.

*For then must He often have suffered since the foundation of the world: but now once in the end of the **world** [aiōn] has He appeared to put away sin by the sacrifice of Himself (Hebrews 9:26).*

*Now all these things happened unto them for examples: and they are written for our admonition, upon whom the ends of the **world** [aiōn] are come (I Corinthians 10:11).*

*And as He sat upon the mount of Olives, the disciples came to Him privately, saying, "Tell us, when shall these things be? and what shall be the sign of Your coming, and of the end of the **world** [aiōn]?" (Matthew 24:3).*

HOW MANY AGES (*AIONS*) ARE THERE?

We can acquire a basic grasp of the number of ages related to God's dealings with man by considering the three basic categories of time: past, present and future. Let's consider three verses that will help us in these three areas of time.

In the Past: *"Even the mystery which has been hidden from **ages** [aiōn] and from generations, but now is made manifest to His saints"* (Colossians 1:26).

In the Present: *"Who gave Himself for our sins, that He might deliver us from this present evil **world** [aiōn], according to the will of God and our Father"* (Galatians 1:4).

In the Future: *"That in the **ages** [aiōn] to come He might show the exceeding riches of His grace in His kindness toward us through Christ Jesus"* (Ephesians 2:7).

In these three verses we have a *minimum* of five ages indicated:

- In Colossians 1:26 we have *"ages"* in the plural form, speaking in the past tense, indicating at least two former ages.
- In Galatians 1:4 we have *"world"* in the singular form, a reference to the present age.
- In Ephesians 2:7, again we have *"ages"* in the plural form, speaking in the future tense, indicating at least two upcoming ages.

This is a *minimum* total of five.

CONCLUSION

In the Scriptures, *"forever,"* *"eternal"* and *"everlasting"* cannot possibly convey the meaning of "endless."

(1) If so, how could *aiōn* ever be in the plural?

(2) If so, how could *aiōn* ever be spoken of as having an end?

The basic concept of *aiōn* does not convey the religious system's imposed definition of "without end." A clear understanding of biblical words, defined by the Scriptures themselves, is always the best remedy to the traditional bondage of the mind, by the doctrines of men.

The fear of the LORD is the beginning of wisdom ...

~ Psalms 111:10

The fear of the LORD is the beginning of knowledge ...

~ Proverbs 1:7

The fear of the LORD is the beginning of wisdom ...

~ Proverbs 9:10

Chapter 11

FEAR
An Elementary Education

One thing that should stand out to us in the three verses above is that fear is only the *"beginning"* of wisdom and knowledge. It is only man's starting place with God, his Creator.

Many miss this important truth, and in doing so, they overlook the pure *elementary* nature of fear. The *"fear of the Lord"* is mankind's first approach to God. It is the awesome discovery of who we really are, and who He really is. It is humanity's approach to God in infancy and immaturity – seeing Him as the righteous almighty One!

Note carefully the first verse that we quoted above, along with the next phase that is to follow:

> *The fear of the LORD is the beginning of wisdom: a good understanding have all they who do His commandments …* (Psalms 111:10).

We see the connection between *"the fear of the Lord"* and doing *"His commandments."* The *"commandments,"* or the *"law,"* is associated with fear.

When God gave *"the law of commandments"* at Sinai the children of Israel *"trembled"* in fear; but the *"law"* and its natural fear in relationship to God was only divine *elementary* education. It was simply a *"schoolmaster"* to bring us to the Lord Jesus Christ (and who among us has not feared the schoolmaster!)

Wherefore the law was our schoolmaster to bring us to Christ, that we might be justified by faith. But after that faith is come, we are no longer under a schoolmaster (Galatians 3:24-25).

Because the "schoolmaster" has brought us to Christ, we are no longer enrolled in its elementary process of *"fear."*

As mature, adult **"sons** of God," our childish, immature **"children** of God" *"fear"* of the Father is replaced by the fullness of *"love."*

Little wonder Paul wrote:

For God has not given us the spirit of fear; but of power, and of love, and of a sound mind (II Timothy 1:7).

Hear these words! *"God has not given us the spirit of fear!"*

God has not given us a place as fearful children. Fear has *no* place in our relationship with the Father. We have been given a place of mature, adult *sonship.* What He has given to us in replacement of elementary *"fear"* is power, love and a sound mind.

John wrote of this as well:

There is no fear in love; but perfect love casts out fear: because fear has torment. He who fears is not made perfect in love (I John 4:18)

Hear these words as well: *"There is no fear in love."* No fear – None!

There is *no* place for *"fear"* in the life of the mature believer, for he has been completely submerged in the glorious love of the Father – *"because the love of God is shed abroad in our hearts by the Holy Spirit which is given to us"* (Romans 5:5).

The very definition of our Father is Love – *"God is Love"* (I John 4:8, 16). He is Love; in fact He is *perfect Love* – and *"perfect love casts out fear."*

Fear and love are exclusive of each other. The issue is one of really knowing Who God is; of actually getting to know *Him.*

Our first approach to God is in ignorance and fear. Then, as we come to know Him in truth – as we become acquainted with His genuine nature of love – fear is driven from our lives, for *"perfect love casts out fear."*

Only those who do not yet know Him, or do not yet know Him very well, fear Him, for *"he who fears is not made perfect in love."*

Now, there are actually three stages related to the *"fear of God"* that we might refer to as:

    Pre-School
    Elementary
    Post-Graduate

We have looked briefly at the last two of these stages. The "Elementary" stage is the early stage of knowing God. It is the acknowledgment that there is a God, and is usually associated with the law (or legalism and religion). This stage is exemplified by those in the "Gospels" who *"were sore afraid"* (*e.g.* Matthew 17:6).

We have also looked at the "Post-Graduate" stage. This is the stage of maturity where the believer no longer lives under the *"the fear of God,"* but enjoys the knowledge of God in fullness. This is the divine goal of perfect love.

There is, however, an earlier, "Pre-School" stage that sometimes is a predecessor of the "Elementary School" stage. For some, this stage comes before the basic knowledge that there is a God. This is the denial or total disregard of God. It is "Pre-School" because it is "pre-law," or "pre-religion." It is the *"fool"* stage that says *"there is no God"* (Psalm 53:1), resulting in *"No fear of God before their eyes"* (Romans 3:18).

We might review these three stages as follows:

Pre-School	Denial or Total Disregard of God	Fool	*"No fear of God before their eyes"*
Elementary	Basic Acknowledgment that there is a God	Infant	*"They were sore afraid"*
Post-Graduate	Knowing God in Fullness	Adult	*"God has not given us the spirit of fear"*

When our Lord Jesus Christ was here on the earth, His most often repeated instruction to those who heard Him was, "Fear Not!" – "Fear Ye Not!" – "Be Not Afraid!" He came to lead others out of fear and into the freedom and peace of love. He lived in a place of perfect Love – that place was His Father.

Getting to know the Father in the reality of His Love will *mature* us out of *"fear"* and into *"perfect love"* – a love that is all-consuming. No wonder Fanny Crosby wrote in her hymn, *Blessed Assurance,* that we are "Filled with His goodness, lost in His Love."

We who really know Him are overtaken by the sea of His divine Love.

Frederick M. Lehman penned his marvelous hymn in 1917:

> The love of God is greater far
> Than tongue or pen can ever tell;
> It goes beyond the highest star,
> And reaches to the lowest hell;
>
> The guilty pair, bowed down with care,
> God gave His Son to win;
> His erring child He reconciled,
> And pardoned from his sin.
>
> When hoary time shall pass away,
> And earthly thrones and kingdoms fall,
> When men who here refuse to pray,
> On rocks and hills and mountains call,

God's love so sure, shall still endure,
All measureless and strong;
Redeeming grace to Adam's race –
The saints' and angels' song.

Could we with ink the ocean fill,
And were the skies of parchment made,
Were every stalk on earth a quill,
And every man a scribe by trade;

To write the love of God above
Would drain the ocean dry;
Nor could the scroll contain the whole,
Though stretched from sky to sky.

Oh, love of God, how rich and pure!
How measureless and strong!
It shall forevermore endure –
The saints' and angels' song.

Are you afraid of the Loving Father? Then you do not yet know Him for who He *really* is. Something of ignorance, religion, and tradition has you bound to a false view of Him.

It is time to know the liberating freedom that is available in the full-growth-knowledge of Him in power, love, and a sound mind.

Saved, yet so as by fire.   ~ I Corinthians 3:15

Chapter 12

SAVED BY FIRE!

Many see God's judgments as an end within themselves, rather than a means to an end. There are coming some wonderful days in the future, days of divine judgment when God shall apply the refiner's fire to His creation. As in the due process of gold and silver's refinement, these days will forever remove all the stains, disgraces and sins of the *"former things."*

Refinement's purging fire is indeed a most gracious act, producing a gloriously positive loss. It will remove all that wishes to be forgotten. As God in His forgiveness remembers them no more, so *"the former things are passed away."*

GOD IS LOVE

God is love (I John 4:8).
God is love (I John 4:16).

John gives us a definitive statement about God. Here we have presented to us the plain, clear definition of God of who He is. Could anything be more direct and to the point?

"God is Love." Love is what He is. Love is who He is. It is not that God's character is simply a loving one; that love is one of His attributes. Neither is it that love is His occasional quality; that sometimes His nature of love gives way to "wrath."

No, indeed not!

God does not simply love: He *is* Love! Love is not just one of His attributes: Love is *who* He is!

Even *"wrath"* is the manifest passion of His love, for Love is who He is, and it is the sum-total of all His ways and workings with His creation. *"Wrath"* and *"judgment"* are not ends unto themselves; they are His wise means to an end – the victorious loving of His creation to Himself.

God Is a Consuming Fire

For our God is a consuming fire (Hebrews 12:29).

We are also told that God is a consuming fire. Is this a contradiction of what John wrote, that He is love? No, indeed not! The same God who is Love is also a consuming fire. He is a consuming fire of divine love. That is the only answer, if Love is who He is.

That God is a *"consuming fire"* wonderfully demonstrates the great passion of His love. His is a *"consuming"* love; and His love is a "purging, purifying" love. His is a love that knows no retreat; knows no end; knows no defeat. He conquers all, not with pure might and strength, not with pure wrath and judgment; but with pure, undying, unrelenting, unceasing, unconditional love.

Love never fails (I Corinthians 13:8).

The greatest of these is love (I Corinthians 13:13).

Love is the greatest, because He is Love – and He is the greatest.

Love never fails, because He is Love – and He never fails.

Saved by Fire

We who know the true and living God, the God of absolute Love, welcome *everything* that comes from His hand, even His *"wrath"* and *"judgment"*; for He *is* Love.

As believers we should welcome the day when our works shall be revealed by *"fire"*; for it is a loving fire that comes from the hands of our Father. He will love away all the dross of our lives.

> *Every man's work shall be made manifest: for the day shall declare it, because it shall be revealed by fire; and the fire shall try every man's work of what sort it is ... If any man's work shall be burned, he shall suffer loss: but he himself shall be saved; yet so as by fire* (I Corinthians 3:13, 15)

We *"shall be saved ... by fire."* This is what Paul wrote. God's fire of love will save us from all the stains and disgraces of the *"former things,"* for *"the former things are passed away."*

Did you ever really stop to consider the glorious nature of the *"fire"* at the Judgment Seat of Christ?[1] Did you ever consider it in relationship to the *"Lake of Fire"* for example?

God's future judgment of believers is associated with "fire."

God's future judgment of unbelievers is associated with "fire."

Fire is such wonderful blessing to our daily lives. We make profitable use of it every day. The only *dangerous* fire – one that is to be feared – is a fire that is *out of control.* Be assured that the God who is Love, and who is a consuming fire – is *not* out of control. As Fanny Crosby wrote in her hymn, He "doeth all things well."

In the Bible fire is presented as having a purging effect. It does so many things – it cleanses, frees, reduces, refines.[2] It is interesting how we recognize this fact when "fire" is applied to the believer, but we forget this when it is applied to the unbeliever. Just as the "fire" of the believer's judgment is a purging, purifying act of God's love; so it is with the "fire" of the unbeliever's judgment.

Think about it! Why do we as believers so often make the *"fire"* of the unbeliever's judgment *literal,* while we leave ours the *figurative* refiner's fire?

The lost will thank God for the *"lake of fire"* that shall free them, and bring to an end their old identity in Adam. This *"lake of fire"* is but the further manifestation

---

1. See the author's work, *The Glorious Presentation of the Saints,* Clyde L. Pilkington, Jr., Bible Student's Press™, (Item #8778).
2. John Wright Follette, *Arrows of Truth.*

of the love of God; of the love of His consuming fire. It is defined by John as *"the second death"* (Revelation 21:8).

Paul teaches us that, *"the last enemy that shall be destroyed is death"* (I Corinthians 15:26). That's what the *"lake of fire"* is – it is *"death."* So it shall be destroyed; and the only way to *"destroy"* death is by *"resurrection!"*

As one former pastor has written:

> As God completes the process of restoring all things (Acts 3:21), all the old rubbish left here by the first Adam (the unrighteous deeds of fallen humanity) will be burned up. Meanwhile, redeemed humanity is welcomed into the presence of God where eventually, *"God shall wipe away all tears from their eyes; and there shall be no more death, neither sorrow, nor crying, neither shall there be any more pain: for the former things are passed away ..."* (Revelation 21:4).
>
> Yes, the Book of Revelation speaks apocalyptically of an *"abyss"* and *"lake of fire,"* but it is in the context of describing the ultimate overthrow of evil.[3]

The lake of fire" is the final death of all evil.

The *"lake of fire"* is just a final death awaiting resurrection.

---

3. Steven L. Rogers, *Quit "Going" to Church ... and Other Musings of a Former Institutional Man*, pages 146-150; 135.

But I would not have you to be ignorant, brothers, concerning them who are asleep, that you sorrow not, even as others who have no hope.

~ I Thessalonians 4:13

Chapter 13

OTHERS WHO HAVE NO HOPE

Q. In I Thessalonians 4:13, Paul refers to *"others which have **no hope**."* If Paul was teaching the Salvation of all, to whom would he be referring as having no hope? In this passage of Scripture it is obvious he is referring to the Resurrection hope, so these *"others"* would not have any hope of resurrection; but how could that be if *"all"* were to be eventually saved?

A. Let's start by getting a definition of the word *"hope."* It is the Greek word *elpis* (*Strong's Greek Lexicon* #1680), and according to Strong it means "expectation or confidence." Interestingly enough it is so identified with faith, that it is even translated as *"faith"* in the *King James Version* (Hebrews 10:23).

We all have neighbors who live around us who are lost. They have no *faith* in the Lord Jesus Christ. As a result they have no *hope* beyond the grave. They believe that the grave is, or may be the end; but just believing it does not make it so. Just because they personally have no hope, does not mean that there is not any hope for them beyond the grave. It simply means that they personally have not the confident expectation (hope) that we do.

Even those who are already saved can be taught incorrectly and thus be without the hope of resurrection. This was the case with some at the city of Corinth. Paul had to write to them about resurrection truth in I Corinthians 15. Here we have believers who had no resurrection hope. Obviously this did not mean that they would not be raised, or that they were "hopeless" beyond the grave.

Hope, as with faith, is a very personal thing. Just because one does not believe in resurrection, does not mean that it does not exist, or that they will not experience it. It just means that they personally have no confident expectation (hope) of it, because of their lack of faith.

Since *"hope"* and *"faith"* are both *King James Version* translations of *"elpis,"* our verse at hand could just as easily have been translated *"others which have no faith."* The reason that they have no hope is that they have no faith.

Believers who have faith and hope in God's promise of resurrection are saved from the hopelessness of the grave, and therefore don't sorrow in the same way as those who do who are without hope.

> *But I would not have you to be ignorant, brothers, concerning them who are asleep, that you sorrow not, even as others who have no hope* (I Thessalonians 4:13).

Just because someone has no hope or faith now, it does not mean that they will not have any in the future. Neither does it mean that the thing to be believed or hoped for does not exist, and that it will not come to pass – even for them.

Hope is a divine quality that is produced in stages. I have more hope now than when I first believed.

> *... Tribulation works patience; and patience, experience; and experience, hope: and hope makes not ashamed; because the love of God is shed abroad in our hearts by the Holy Spirit which is given to us* (Romans 5:3-5).

Hope is a process. Starting with tribulation, and then through experience, finally hope is produced in our lives. This divine process has not yet been fully developed in the lost. God is not now working with the full harvest; He is working with the firstfruit. The full harvest has no personal hope within the heart at this time; but not to worry, for the end result is not about man at all, but about God Himself, *"Who worketh all things after the counsel of His own will"* (Ephesians 1:11).

The simple fact is that God has subjected the entire creation to hope, and it shall be delivered from the bondage of corruption, whether or not they apprehend it by faith (hope) now.

> *For the creature was made subject to vanity, not willingly, but by reason of Him Who has subjected the same in hope, because the creature itself also shall be delivered from the bondage of corruption into the glorious liberty of the children of God. For we know that the whole creation groans and travails in pain together until now. And not only they, but ourselves also, who have the firstfruits of the Spirit, even we ourselves groan within ourselves, waiting for the adoption, to wit, the redemption of our body* (Romans 8:20-23).

The same *"creature"* that was *"made subject to vanity"* is the exact same *"creature"* that shall *"be delivered from the bondage of corruption into the glorious liberty of the children of God."* This is why Paul refers to *"the whole creation,"* of which we are but *"the firstfruits of the Spirit."*

This is the *"subjection"* of divine hope upon *"the whole creation."*

The same *"all men"* who were condemned in Adam are the exact same *"all men"* who will be justified in Christ.

> *Therefore as by the offence of one judgment came upon all men to condemnation; even so by the righteousness of One the free gift came upon all men unto justification of life* (Romans 5:18).

The same *"many"* who were made sinners in Adam are the exact same *"many"* who will be made righteous in Christ.

> *For as by one man's disobedience many were made sinners, so by the obedience of One shall many be made righteous* (Romans 5:19).

The same *"all"* who die in Adam are the exact same *"all"* who will be made alive in Christ.

> *For as in Adam all die, even so in Christ shall all be made alive* (I Corinthians 15:22).[1]

---

1. The verse does *not* read, *"For as all those who are in Adam die, even so also all those who are in Christ shall be made alive."*

Be not overcome of evil, but overcome evil with good.

~ Romans 12:21

Chapter 14

THE ERROR OF ETERNAL CONSCIOUS TORMENT:
Its Effect on the Conscience of the Believer

I have received a lot of correspondence concerning the subject of the salvation of all mankind. Some have written of their enlightenment after having read the material in this book as it originally appeared in the pages of the *Bible Student's Notebook*™.

Then of course there have been those who have not agreed with what has been written. Overwhelmingly these have been good-spirited. Interestingly one recurring theme shows up in many of these letters. It is the confession that the writers wish they believed in the salvation of all.

"I WOULD LOVE TO BELIEVE"

Here are a few excerpts from four recent letters. I find these lines very touching. Read these short lines carefully and see if you cannot identify with the words written. See if they don't express something that has been in your own heart.

"I do not see the reconciliation of all mankind. I wish I did. It would be great if all these lost souls would someday come to the truth."

"Don't get me wrong, I would LOVE to believe there is no hell and that everyone gets saved in the end. I don't like the idea of Hell and I don't understand how or why God would send anyone to a place like that. Doesn't seem fair at all

... I would like nothing more than to find out you are correct in your beliefs in this area."

"I'd really like to believe that all will be saved. I have a real hard time with someone in eternal torments."

"I have *never* been comfortable with eternal punishment in fire for the lost. It has always haunted me that God could torture lost souls in fire forever."

These four brothers in Christ are not alone. The erroneous teaching of "eternal conscious torment" has an affect upon the conscience of the believer. Buried deep within our conscious – in our subconscious – is this part of "God" that we do not like. It is so unlike Him. It is so unlike who He wants us to be. We do not like this "dark side" of "God."

As we have come to see in this short work, this "god" with a dark side is not the true God of Scriptures. This eternally sadistic "god" is one of religion. The true God of the Scriptures is good. His very nature is love, grace, forbearance, and forgiveness. He is far greater than we ever imagined Him to be.

The point here is that this religious teaching of "eternal conscious torment" has an adverse effect upon the very conscience of the believer. It obstructs his true understanding of his Father, inhibits the enjoyment of his relationship with Him, and skews the way he sees and relates to all the rest of God's dear creatures.

THE TESTIMONY OF BIBLE TEACHERS

Other sincere brethren have not held to the salvation of all, but have nonetheless also written concerning their own personal anguish over the issue also.

Albert Barnes, the famous biblical commentator (*Barnes' Notes*) describes well such agony of spirit:

> That any should suffer forever, lingering on in hopeless despair, and rolling amidst infinite torments without the possibility of alleviation and without end; that since God can save men and will save a part, He has not proposed to save all – these are real, not imaginary, difficulties. ...

My whole soul pants for light and relief on these questions. But I get neither; and in the distress and anguish of my own spirit, I confess that I see no light whatever. I see not one ray to disclose to me why sin came into the world; why the earth is strewn with the dying and the dead; and why man must suffer to all eternity. I have never seen a particle of light thrown on these subjects, that has given a moment's ease to my tortured mind. ...

I confess, when I look on a world of sinners and sufferers – upon death-beds and grave-yards upon the world of woe filled with hosts to suffer for ever: when I see my friends, my family, my people, my fellow citizens when I look upon a whole race, all involved in this sin and danger – and when I see the great mass of them wholly unconcerned, and when I feel that God only can save them, and yet he does not do so, I am struck dumb. It is all dark, dark, dark to my soul, and I cannot disguise it. – Albert Barnes, *Practical Sermons*, (page 123).

Even **Sir Robert Anderson** lends his voice to this dilemma:

According to the most careful estimate, the population of the world exceeds one thousand four hundred millions. Not one-third of these are Christians even in name; and of this small minority how few there are whose lives give proof that they are traveling heavenward! And what is the destiny of all the rest? Any estimate of their number must be inaccurate and fanciful; and accuracy, if attainable, would be practically useless. As a matter of arithmetic it is as easy to deal with millions as with tens; but when we come to realize that every unit is a human being, with a little world of joys and sorrows all his own, and an unbounded capacity for happiness or misery, the mind is utterly paralyzed by the effort to realize the problem.

And these fourteen hundred millions are but a single wave of the great tide of human life that breaks, generation after generation, upon the shore of the unknown world. What future then awaits these untold myriads of millions of mankind? Most of us have been trained in the belief that their portion is an existence of endless, hopeless torment. But few there are, surely, who have carried this belief to middle-age unchallenged. Sometimes it is the vastness of the numbers whose fate is involved that startles us into skepticism. Sometimes it is the memory of friends now gone, who lived and died impenitent. As we think of an eternity in which they '*shall be tormented day and night forever and ever,*' the mind grows weary and the heart grows sick, and we turn to ask ourselves, Is not God infinite in love? Is not the great Atonement infinite in value? Is it credible then that such a future is to be the sequel to a brief and sorely tempted life of sin? Is it credible that for all eternity – that eternity in which the triumph of the Cross shall be complete, and God shall be 'all in all' – there shall still remain an underworld of seething sin and misery and horror? – Sir Robert Anderson, *Human Destiny*, (Chapter 5: The Restitution of All Things).

Even more recently Mart De Haan wrote:

> I wish I didn't have to believe in hell. While seeing the need for eternal justice, the thought of cruel and unusual punishment that lasts forever sounds morally wrong to me ... – Mart De Haan, *Radio Bible Class* Newsletter, (November 2006).

ARE WE MORE KIND, GRACIOUS AND LOVING THAN GOD?

Is it possible for the redeemed to be more kind, gracious and loving than their God? Deep in our innermost beings we cannot honestly fathom the concept of *"eternal conscious torment."* Its cruelty and callousness is terrible beyond comprehension. Even though some may teach it, very few have given their minds the permission to dwell upon it in its fullness.

Yet the fact is that we are *not* more kind, gracious, and loving than our heavenly Father.

He Is Love

> *God is love* (I John 4:8b).

His Love Will Never Fail

> *Love never fails* (I Corinthians 13:8a).

He Teaches Us to Be Like Him, and to Love Our Enemies

> *Love your enemies, do good to them who hate you ... Be therefore merciful, as your Father also is merciful* (Luke 6:27, 36).

He Teaches Us to Forgive Them Infinitely

"How often shall my brother sin against me, and I forgive him? Until seven times?" Jesus said to him, "I say not to you, until seven times: but, until seventy times seven" (Matthew 18:21-22).

He Teaches Us Not to Be Overcome by Evil, but to Overcome Evil by Good

Be not overcome of evil, but overcome evil with good (Romans 12:21).

Our Father Teaches Us These Things Because They Are Who He Is

Religion has grossly misrepresented God. Those who have professed to be in His service have done His honor a disservice. He has been exceedingly slandered.

God is Good Beyond Our Wildest Dreams

O give thanks unto the LORD; for He is good; for His mercy endures forever (I Chronicles 16:34).

... For He is good; for His mercy endures forever ... (II Chronicles 5:13).

... For He is good; for His mercy endures forever (II Chronicles 7:3).

Praise the LORD. O give thanks unto the LORD; for He is good: for His mercy endures forever (Psalm 106:1).

O give thanks unto the LORD, for He is good: for His mercy endures forever (Psalm 107:1).

O give thanks unto the LORD; for He is good: because His mercy endures forever (Psalm 118:1).

O give thanks unto the LORD; for He is good: for His mercy endures forever (Psalm 118:29).

O give thanks unto the LORD; for He is good: for His mercy endures forever (Psalm 136:1).

Then Paul stood in the midst of Mars' Hill, and said, "You men of Athens, I perceive that in all things you are too superstitious. For as I passed by, and beheld your devotions, I found an altar with this inscription, 'TO THE UNKNOWN GOD.' Whom therefore you ignorantly worship, Him declare I to you. God Who made the world and all things therein, seeing that He is Lord of heaven and earth, dwells not in temples made with hands; neither is worshiped with men's hands, as though He needed anything, seeing He gives to all life, and breath, and all things; and has made of one blood all nations of men for to dwell on all the face of the earth, and has determined the times before appointed, and the bounds of their habitation; that they should seek the Lord, if haply they might feel after Him, and find Him, though He is not far from every one of us: for in Him we live, and move, and have our being; as certain also of your own poets have said, 'For we are also His offspring.' Forasmuch then as we are the offspring of God, we ought not to think that the Godhead is like unto gold, or silver, or stone, graven by art and man's device. And the times of this ignorance God winked at; but now commands all men everywhere to repent: because He has appointed a day, in the which He will judge the world in righteousness by that Man whom He has ordained; whereof He has given assurance unto all men, in that He has raised Him from the dead.

~ Acts 17:22-31

Chapter 15

PAUL'S NEGLECTED MESSAGE
Mars Hill (Acts 17)

Even among those who place a great emphasis on Paul, with his unique apostleship and message, there is an amazing neglect of one of his most outstanding messages found in the Book of Acts. I am referring to his message given on Mars' Hill in Acts chapter 17.

There seems to be a great familiarity with the first account that is reported in this chapter: Paul at the city of Berea, with those who nobly searched the Scriptures daily. But when it comes to the next city that Paul encounters, it does not get as much attention as it should.

Paul moved on from Berea to Athens, and while there he gave one of his most remarkable addresses. The content of his message to this group of unbelieving pagans has been far too long overlooked. These words of Paul contain a very rich message. Preserved in the Scriptures, we know that it not only was a challenge to the pagans of Athens, but that it will prove to be a challenge to the members of Christ's Body as well. The real challenge for us in the message that he gave will be whether or not we even have an adequate perception of Paul's core message at all.

No Reference to Scripture

We will not be taking an exhaustive look at Acts 17:22-31 by any means. Neither do I intend that we do so. What I desire to do in this short study is to simply cast a little light upon some of the neglected things that Paul declared. This means that we will deliberately pass over many wonderful statements of Paul. Do not allow this reading to be your end of the matter. Study the entire passage for yourself – not missing one morsel of greatness that is contained in it.

Before proceeding, we will take the opportunity to note what Paul did *not* say in his important talk. One of the most significant things about this entire message is the complete absence of any use of Scripture. Not even once does Paul quote the Scriptures. Maybe just as interesting, the only quotation by Paul is one of a heathen poet.

What is so extremely striking about this is that we are often taught that the God-honoring method of communicating with the lost (*i.e.,* "witnessing," "soul winning," "preaching," etc.) is to riddle our "messages" with Scripture references. In some circles, one's spirituality may even be judged based upon the amount of Scripture memorized and delivered during such an "evangelistic" opportunity.

Really, think about it, can you even image Paul addressing lost pagans and never even reciting a passage from Scripture? If we had such an opportunity ourselves, many of us would surely believe that we were unfaithful and negligent if we "failed" to use as much of the Bible as we possibly could.

Not that sharing the Scriptures is never to be done with the lost, for surely Paul did. But maybe we should learn a little something from Paul here, and not make our conversations with the lost such a *rote and quote* of Scripture. Maybe, like Paul, we should simply seek to find a place of identification with them – in something that they know and understand – something that is in their frame of reference – something that is important to them; just as he did with their idol to the *"Unknown God,"* and their heathen poetry.

Maybe we should learn to talk to our "Athenians" about sports, movies and other cultural and social interests that they may have, and in these things interpret a divine meaning to life, just as Paul did with the people in his day.

Paul Vieira, in his book *Jesus Has Left the Building,* encourages us along these lines, in what he refers to as cultural literacy:

> We have learned to live without contact with the world. We have created an artificial environment that goes beyond the simplicity of Christian community … With its own language and customs, in many cases those who enter this "church culture" from the outside encounter a form of culture shock …
>
> How well can you read the culture? Do you know how to speak the language of culture? Do you really understand the person with whom you work or go to school? What is the cry in the heart of people who live on your street? They are not going to speak to you in the same way a believer does. Our ability to understand the worldviews of others will enable us to more effectively communicate with them. Culture is the teacher of worldviews and gives the language with which we are able to speak …
>
> Although as Christians we abide in a new culture called *the Kingdom of God,* we must still know the culture that surrounds us. We are in the world, but not of it. If we are going to be effective in communicating … to those who move within the limits of their culture, we must be able to speak to them in a language they can understand …
>
> What aided the apostles in establishing a voice to the people of their culture was that they knew how to adjust their language according to who was listening. An illustration of this can be found in chapter seventeen of the book of Acts … Paul did some homework during his stay in Athens …
>
> Could it be that there are people in our lives who are longing to connect with God but just don't know how? Are there things about our culture that provide a springboard for the gospel to be preached and demonstrated? I believe that God has provided exit doors in every culture around the world. These are subtle passageways to finding God, where culture and *the Kingdom of God* intersect. We can possess the insight to locate these portals. They are simply the entry points that provide opportunity for us to share Christ.
>
> Often these entry points are found in the artistic parts of culture. Paul understood this when he quoted the Greek poets in his message that day on Mars' Hill; *"As certain also of your own poets have said, For we are also His offspring"* (Acts 17:28). It's interesting to note that Paul doesn't quote the Bible

once in his appeal to the Athenians. They would not have had any point of reference in regards to the Hebrew Scriptures. Paul must have researched the writing of the Greek philosophers and poets in order to be able to speak to that culture. Paul used their own trusted sources as a basis of presenting the gospel of Jesus to those people.

Who are the trusted sources of our culture? Stephen Spielberg, John Lennon, Sting, Michael Jordan, Bono, Eminem, Jennifer Lopez, Larry and Andy Wachowski, J.R.R. Tolkien, and George Lucas, to name only a few. These are the poets, musicians, artists and storytellers of our time. Whether you agree with it or not, these are the trusted sources of our culture. Hidden in the songs, books, movies, sporting events, and cultural phenomena are gateways. Thoughts, ideas, statements, pictures and metaphors that line up with truth in the gospel message are waiting to be interpreted and proclaimed. The followers of Jesus are the interpreters of the divine revelation that God is speaking through culture. Without us, the truth lies there undiscovered. The precious goes unnoticed in the heap of the worthless.

Paul's approach on Mars' Hill is very helpful for believers … Paul presents God in an all encompassing way. He is not merely the God of a specific religion or ethnicity; the true and living God is the God of all people. Christians these days are often viewed as being narrow-minded and exclusive …

Paul debunked the understanding that God could be contained in buildings by his statement, *"God that made the world and all things therein, seeing that he is Lord of heaven and earth, dwelleth not in temples made with hands"* (Acts 17:24). Paul preached a God that was outside the building … Paul's God was universal and near to every human heart on the planet.

Now we shall begin our brief journey into some of the neglected aspects of Paul's message to those on Mars' Hill.

THE UNKNOWN GOD

Ignorant Worship

Whom therefore you ignorantly worship, Him declare I unto you.

Paul begins to talk with them regarding something about which they evidently had an extreme interest: idols. The interesting thing is what he said to them. He said that they worshiped God – the true and living God – but that they just did so ignorantly.

> *Whom therefore you **ignorantly** worship, Him declare I unto you.*

He wanted to talk to them about the God that they worshiped, although ignorantly. The word *"ignorantly"* is an adverb that tells us *how* they worshiped God. They worshiped Him for sure – it was simply done in *ignorance!* So said Paul.

Think of that. If we had been there with Paul, would we have accused the Athenians of not worshiping God at all, because they did so before idols?

Let's bring this into our own culture. Would we accuse Catholics (or those of various Protestant denominations) of not worshiping God, just because they might do so ignorantly? Do they not indeed worship, just like those on Mars' Hill, even if it is in ignorance?

What about Jehovah's Witnesses, or Mormons? What about Jews? Or, dare we say Muslims? Could these be any "worse" worshipers than the idol worshiping men of Athens? Is it not true that they worship God, just ignorantly?

What a different perspective this has on things! Paul said "let me tell you about Him!" This would surely seem like high-heresy to one raised in Christian fundamentalism. I know. I would never have thought I would see things this way; but here we have the very words and example of Paul himself.

Those who *"worship"* in ignorance, nonetheless worship the true and living God; thankfully, ignorance is curable – and sooner or later *"every knee shall bow, and every tongue shall confess to God"* (Romans 14:11).

The truth of this would do away with denominational and religious division and hostility in the heart of the believer. I do not speak here of ecumenicalism, but of being outside of the religious barriers and bondage, and being free to love and accept others, exactly where they are.

Not in Man-Made Temples

Seeing that He is Lord of heaven and earth, dwells not in temples made with hands.

Why, this statement would manage to get most of Christendom stirred all out of sorts; but it's true: God does not live in man-made structures of any kind.

Would Paul count our contemporary Christianity – with its "House of God" and "Sanctuary" – among the likes of the pagan temples of Athens? Are not these Christian "Houses of Worship" just as pagan, and as heathen as those of Athens?

Yet there is really *good news* in all of this. God does not live in humanly devised architecture. We do not need to "go" somewhere to "meet" Him. For truly,

In Him we live, and move, and have our being.[1]

THE NEARNESS OF GOD

The reason that there is no need for man-made temples (or other places of worship) is because God is already near to all of us.

Kinship of Man

He … has made of one blood all nations of men for to dwell on all the face of the earth.

Paul taught that all men are of the same family – *"of one blood."* The truth of this would do away with social and racial division and hostility in the heart of the believer.

Feeling After God

*If haply they might **feel** after Him.*

Some of our brands of Christianity could not appreciate these words of Paul. Men were designed and placed by God in a way that they *"might feel after Him."*

---

1. See *Where on Earth Is God?*, Clyde L. Pilkington, Jr., *Bible Student's Notebook* #45.

Christianity-in-a-Box is often quick to discount the work of God in the lives of those outside of its own group-norm. God's drawing of mankind is a lifelong – and even beyond that (in resurrection) – work. We must not be too quick to pass judgment on those who, in ignorance, nevertheless *"might feel after Him."*

Not Far from Everyone

Though He is not far from every one of us.

We would not have been surprised if we had read this spoken to the righteous, godly Ephesians; but this was not spoken to them. We don't find this message recorded in the letter to the Ephesians, or to any other group of saints for that matter. No, this was spoken to lost, pagan Athenians!

We like to think of God as being very "near" to us (and our group), but so very "far" from them (and their group); but the fact is that Paul told the pagans of Athens that God is *"not far from **every one of us.**"*

Paul's message was that God is near to **"every one,"** but that is not all. Paul did not say, "every one of YOU;" He said, **"every one of US."** Paul placed himself – along with the Athenians – in the single, worldwide class *"us"* of mankind.

God is close to all of "us." This is because,

God was in Christ, **reconciling the world to Himself** (II Corinthians 5:19).

The truth of this would do away with the "us" and "them" division and hostility in the heart of the believer.

We Live in Him

In Him we live, and move, and have our being.

Again, we would not have been surprised to have read this spoken to the Ephesians, but this too was spoken to unbelievers. One can hardly believe it, and we would not, if it were not from the very mouth of Paul, our apostle.

The simple fact is that *all* men are ALREADY in the presence of God; we *live* there! It is not some place that we "go": it is some place that we simply "are." He is where we – all of us – live and move and have our being.

What a wonderful thing it is to *"live"* in the Father. What an amazing thing it is to *"move"* in Him. What an astonishing thing it is to *"have our being"* in Him.

Each and every one of us has the privilege to live in the REALITY of this union with our Father – as each new day begins and unfolds. What a blessed thing to be in constant communion with Him – heart to heart. This union is ALREADY *fully* ours, secured and maintained by *His* very own nature.

What an impact upon our lives this would have if we were only to embrace it in simple faith.

THE FATHERHOOD OF GOD

God's Offspring

For we are also His offspring.

Again, this is not spoken to believers, but to pagan unbelievers.

Can we believe that Paul would say this? We would not bat an eye if it were said of saints; but for Paul to quote a pagan poet, and then verify that in truth *"we"* – again Paul grouping himself *with them* – are all the offspring of God, is absolutely astounding.

As certain also of your own poets have said, "For we are also His offspring." Forasmuch then as we are the offspring of God …

Paul's point is unmistakable. The word *"offspring"* here is also translated in the *King James Version* as "kindred" (Acts 4:6; 7:19), "of the stock" (Acts 13:26; Philippians 3:5), and *"born"* (Acts 18:2, 24).

Just think of it! *"The offspring of God."* Could we even have fathomed such a worldwide declaration as *"we are the offspring of God"*?

Following the *King James* translational suit, we have,

> *we are the **offspring** of God*
> *we are the **kindred** of God*
> *we are of the **stock** of God*
> *we are the **born** of God*

Let's have the courage of faith, then, that we, too, along with Paul, can tell those whom we meet that they belong to God, that they are His children, and that He – *in truth* – is their Father.

The truth of this would also surely do away with all manner of division and hostility in the heart of the believer.

THE SOVEREIGNTY OF GOD

Repentance

> *God … now commands all men everywhere to repent.*

The Pauline call to *"repentance"* is the call to rethink everything we think we know in light of the truth of God. It is the call to accept the divine viewpoint over the human viewpoint – a radical change of mind.[2]

In the context of Paul's words here, he is telling his hearers that their Father is enjoining[3] them to have a change of mind about Him! Surely the words of Paul to the Athenians constituted a completely different way of thinking! This repentance was not just needed for the men on Mars' Hill. I suggest that even for those who *think* we know our Bible today, we are finding that we too, are in many ways worshiping a God that we do not know very well, that we have been quite ignorant of Him ourselves.

---

2. The word *"repent"* here is *Strong's Greek Lexicon* #3340 *"metanoeo,"* meaning, "to think differently … *i.e.,* reconsider."

   The word *repent,* from the Greek word *metanoia,* actually means a change of mind – a radical revision and transformation of our whole mental process … receiving a new mind. – Jim Palmer, *Wide Open Spaces* (2007), p. 75.
3. The word *"commandeth"* is *Strong's Greek Lexicon* #3853 *"paraggello,"* meaning "to transmit a message, *i.e.,* (by implication) to enjoin."

   Noah Webster says of *enjoin:* "as a parent enjoins on his children the duty of obedience" – *American Dictionary of the English Language,* 1828.

Worldwide Righteousness

Judge the world in righteousness.

We are often led to think of the word *"judge"* as a term of condemnation. The fact is that the word for *"judge"* simply means to "rule." It is the same Greek word translated *"judging"* in Matthew 19:28, where the Twelve Apostles will sit on twelve thrones, *"judging"* (ruling; governing) the Twelve tribes of Israel. It is just in the same manner that Old Testament Israel had *"Judges"* in the past as their national leaders.[4]

For now, *"the whole world lies in wickedness"* (I John 5:19); but,

> *He has appointed a day, in the which He will judge* [govern] *the world in righteousness by that Man* [the Lord Jesus Christ] *Whom He has ordained; whereof He has given assurance unto* ALL MEN, *in that He has raised Him from the dead* (Acts 17:31).

Faith to All Men

He has given assurance unto all men.

The word *"assurance"* here is so translated only twice in the *King James Version* from the Greek word *pistis;*[5] but it is translated 241 times as *"faith."*

Thus, the *Concordant Version* translates it as,

*Tendering **faith** to all.*

Tyndale translated it,

Faith *to all men.*

God has "given *faith* unto all men" – *"according as God has dealt to every man the measure of faith"* (Romans 12:3). It is the blindness of *ignorance* that keeps this faith from embracing the true nature of its Father. One day, the ignorance will be completely dispelled and this *"faith"* will *"repent"* (think differently), so,

---

4. The word *"judge"* here is *Strong's Greek Lexicon* #2919 *"krino,"* meaning "to distinguish, *i.e.,* decide."
5. *Strong's Greek Lexicon* #4102, translated *"faith."*

That at the name of Jesus every knee should bow, of things in heaven, and things in earth, and things under the earth; and that every tongue should confess that Jesus Christ is Lord, to the glory of God the Father (Philippians 2:10-11).

What a message of hope. What a message of confident assurance. Paul's message on Mars' Hill faithfully represents the glorious *good news* given to him for all mankind of God's work in His Son, the Lord Jesus Christ.

The Gospel of our Lord and Savior, Jesus Christ, committed to Paul the Apostle, is truly better *good news* than any of us could ever have imagined! It is far more glorious than religion would ever have us believe!

God's purpose of the ages will not be complete until His full creative bounty is restored so that He is *"All **IN** all"* (I Corinthians 15:28).

I trust that you will be at liberty to set aside religious paradigms and enjoy the amazing riches of Christ's finished cross-work!

All things are of God, Who has reconciled us to Himself by Jesus Christ, and has given to us the ministry of reconciliation; to wit [that is], that God was in Christ, reconciling the world to Himself, not imputing their trespasses to them; and has committed to us the Word of reconciliation.

~ II Corinthians 5:18-19

Chapter 16

WORLD RECONCILIATION

What absolutely amazing words from Paul, God's apostle to the nations! What a divine revelation was committed to his trust. Oh, for the faith to fully believe the disclosure of the divine plan. Oh, for the courage to embrace God's full accomplishments in the reconciliatory work of the Lord Jesus Christ!

II Corinthians Chapter 5 is a glorious revelation of what God consummated in His Son. It is an exceedingly rich presentation by God's apostle of grace. Here we learn of the full scope of reconciliation.

WORLDWIDE RECONCILIATION

Reconciling the world *to Himself* (:19).

What was the revelation given to Paul, about God's work in Christ? What did he reveal that God actually accomplished in Christ?

Reconciliation!

Hear that word. God procured *"reconciliation"* through His Son.

Just what is *"reconciliation"*? It is the restoration to divine favor.[1] The enmity, division and estrangement of man towards God have been removed by the Father Himself – *"reconciling the world to Himself."*

It was indeed true that,

> *When we were enemies, we were **reconciled to God** by the death of His Son* (Romans 5:10).

The same word that Paul uses for *"reconciliation"* (:18-19), is translated in the very next verse in the *King James Version* as *"atonement"* (the old English "at-one-ment"):

> *We also joy in God through our Lord Jesus Christ, by Whom we have now received the **atonement** [at-one-ment]* (Romans 5:11).[2]

What a work of reconciliation – atonement – restoration. Nothing stands between the Father and His creation.

For whom did God accomplish this work in Christ?

The World!

> *Reconciling **the world*** (:19).

> *The reconciling of **the world*** (Romans 11:15).

> *Reconcile **all things** to Himself* (Colossians 1:20).

Reconciliation was not just for a few – it was not just believers who were restored to God – the scope of Christ's atoning work was revealed by Paul to be *worldwide!*

The far-reaching, triumphant cross-work of Jesus Christ was not limited to those who currently believe. He was not partial in His work and accomplishments. He was all-inclusive. Christ did His wonderful work for the whole world.

---

1. *Strong's Greek Lexicon* #2643 *"katallage,"* meaning "restoration to (the divine) favor." Noah Webster defines the root of reconciliation (conciliate) as, "to unite." (*American Dictionary of the English Language*, 1828).
2. Or, as other translations have, *"received the **reconciliation"*** (*American Standard Version, J.N. Darby's Translation, Young's Literal Translation*).

DIVINE RECONCILIATION

*Reconciling the world **to Himself*** (:19).

*Reconcile all things **to Himself*** (Colossians 1:20).

This reconciliation is not man's work in any sense. Man is not restoring himself to God; man is not coming to God; but God is coming to man, in Christ: *"that God was in Christ, reconciling the world **to Himself."***

The world did not reconcile *itself* to God. Instead, it was the Father Who reconciled the world to Himself. He did so without any effort or merit on man's part, for He did the work of reconciliation while the world was still His *"enemy."* He reconciled the world to Himself by the death of His dear Son.

Reconciliation – the restoration to divine favor – is purely a divine work. It does not take place by *any* effort whatsoever on man's part. The Father *"Himself"* did the work through the *at-one-ment* of His Son, the Lord Jesus Christ. The world has now been made at-one with the Father.

NON-IMPUTATION OF SIN

Not imputing their trespasses to them (:19).

Just what does this worldwide reconciliation involve? It involves the trespasses of the world against Him; and that He is not imputing them. This is an amazing revelation of truth committed to Paul; a revolutionary doctrine in contrast to record-keeping orthodoxy.

Most of Christendom could not even fathom that the believer's sins are not being *"imputed"* (Romans 4:8); let alone that the work of Christ has obtained something on a far grander scale. When Paul says, *"Not imputing their trespasses to them,"* *"them"* is a reference to the *"the world."* Paul taught that God was not imputing the world's trespasses!

Just what is *"imputation"*? It is record-keeping. It is the bookkeeping process of accounting, or numbering. [3]

---

3. *Strong's Greek Lexicon* #3049, *logizomai,* meaning "to take an inventory." Some of the other ways that it is translated in the *King James Version* are: count, account, number and reckon.

   Noah Webster defines *"impute"* as, "to charge; to attribute; to set to the account of ... we impute crimes, sins, trespasses, faults, blame, &c., to the guilty persons." (*American Dictionary of the English Language,* 1828)

Paul is telling us that God does not tally man's trespasses against him. He does not record them. He does not keep an account of them. He does not charge them to one's record. This is because,

Christ died for our sins (I Corinthians 15:3),

and,

Because ... if One died for all, then were all dead (II Corinthians 5:14).[4]

MINISTRY AND WORD OF RECONCILIATION

*Has given to us the **ministry of reconciliation** ... Has committed to us the **Word of reconciliation*** (:18-19).

What a change of attitude reconciliation is from the religious mindset and worldview.

We, as *first-trusters*,[5] have the privilege of enjoying this reconciliation, living in the realization of divine favor, that nothing stands between us and the Father.

God has given the *first-trusters* a ministry. We are the Father's *"vessels of mercy"* (Romans 9:23); we are to see all men in their relationship to this all-inclusive

---

4. Or, as other translations have:

that One died for all, therefore all died (*The Holy Bible in Modern English*, 1903, Ferrar Fenton)

that if One for all died, then the whole died (*Young's Literal Translation,* 1863, Robert Young).

5. *That we should be to the praise of His glory, who **first trusted** in Christ* (Ephesians 1:12).

Do not be discouraged as you look around you. What you see is not the end of God's plan and purpose. Granted, the world is filled with sin and unbelief – that *"the whole world lies in wickedness"* (I John 5:19) – but God is not yet done. Don't judge the final outcome by the current state of things. This is not the finished product of God.

God has not saved us simply to abandon the rest of mankind in eternal torment. We are just the *first-trusters,* the *firstfruits* of Christ's glorious redemptive work. Ultimately God's plan includes *all* of His creation. None will be permanently lost. Divine love never fails to reach its goal.

Those of us who now trust the Lord Jesus Christ are but the beginning of God's glorious work. We are but the *first-trusters* in His glorious design.

In every harvest there is that small portion of the crop that matures early, before the vast majority of the rest. The *firstfruits* are a token of that which is to come – the full harvest.

Under the Old Testament economy the *firstfruits* belonged to God, and were holy unto Him.

In every generation, and in every place, God has had His *firstfruits;* those that come to harvest earlier than the rest. What a blessed privilege to be the *firstfruits* of the Lord, and just as God has brought us to faith, He too will bring the rest of His creation.

What a joy to be in on God's *early* plans! As a part of the *firstfruits* of the harvest we have so much for which to be thankful. We are especially thrilled when we think how our Father has made us co-laborers with Him in His sovereign plan to include all of His creation in His full harvest.

reconciliation of God. Our ministry is not institutional, nor organizational; it is simply to share with those around us the Father's love and acceptance of them through the person of the Lord Jesus Christ. We only entreat them,

in Christ's stead, **Be reconciled to God** (II Corinthians 5:20).

We are not encouraging them to "do" anything; but to simply *"be"* what the Father has already made them: *"reconciled to God."*

That which is committed to us is not the "ministry of condemnation," nor the "ministry of retribution," nor the "ministry of judgment" – rather, it is the *"ministry of reconciliation."*

Ours is not the "word of wrath," nor the "word of punishment," nor the "word of damnation" – rather, it is the *"Word of reconciliation."*

Our very lives – even down to the nature and intent of what proceeds out of our mouths – are to be the embodiment of the Father's reconciliation work in Christ Jesus.

Let your speech be always with grace, *seasoned with salt, that you may know how you ought to answer every man* (Colossians 4:6).[6]

ULTIMATE REALIZATION

The world has been *unioned* with the Father. He has removed all enmity, division and estrangement. Through Christ the world has been brought into the fullness of divine favor.

Not all of the world has this knowledge at this time. They are still *"alienated and enemies,"* but this condition exists ONLY in **their** minds (Colossians 1:21).[7]

---

6. Note that Paul does not say "**what** ye ought to answer" – but *"**how** you ought to answer."* How? *"always with grace!"* ... *"That it may minister grace to the hearers"* (Ephesians 4:29).

7.   *And you, who were sometime alienated and enemies **in your mind** by wicked works, yet now has He reconciled.*

   Interestingly the word that is translated *"reconciled"* here is *Strong's Greek Lexicon* #604 *apokatallasso,* which is a compound word from #575 and #2644, meaning "to reconcile fully."

   This is the word that is used in Colossians 1:20:

   *And, having made peace through the blood of His cross, by Him to **reconcile** all things to Himself; by Him, I say, whether they are things in earth, or things in heaven.*

   By Paul's use of the word here, we can see that *"all things"* will indeed one day be *"fully reconciled"* to Him. This "full reconciliation" takes place when the *mental alienation* is finally removed in all of creation.

This is not how things *really* are now. The world only needs to be brought to the realization of their reconciliation, and this *will* come in due course.

The Father has already *made* all men reconciled to Himself. Now, men only need to **"be"** what He has made them – *"reconciled to God."* In our Father's own good course of time, all will indeed **"be** *reconciled to God."*

Until that time, ours is truly a *good news* ministry; and we are privileged to live in the spirit of divine reconciliation – allowing it to permeate our attitudes, hearts and lives. In the spirit of our Father, we are free to live in personal reconciliation among ourselves and with others.

That at the name of Jesus every knee should bow, of things in heaven, and things in earth, and things under the earth; and that every tongue should confess that Jesus Christ is Lord, to the glory of God the Father (Philippians 2:10-11).

When they were filled, He said to His disciples, "Gather up the fragments that remain, **that nothing is lost."**

~ John 6:12

Chapter 17

NOTHING WILL BE LOST!
The Reconciliation of *All* Things, *Including* Satan and the Fallen Celestial Powers

*A*fter our Lord Jesus Christ miraculously had fed the *"five thousand,"*[1] there was still food remaining. He had made provision beyond the present time; and instructed His disciples to collect the leftovers so *"that nothing be lost."*

Albert Barnes (1798–1870), in his commentary of Scripture, wrote regarding this account:

> It shows the care of Jesus that there should be no waste. Though He had power to provide any quantity of God, yet He has here taught us that the bounties of Providence are not to be squandered. In all things the Savior set us an example … If *He* was thus saving, it becomes us dependent creatures not to waste the bounties of a beneficent Providence … The loaves and fishes created by the Savior were His gift … not given them to waste … Everything should be applied to its appropriate end, and nothing should be squandered or lost.[2]

What rich lessons we learn from the earthly life and ministry of our precious Savior. He was here revealing the true nature and character of our Father; and what a simple and yet far-reaching principle we learn here: the heart of the Father is *"that nothing be lost."*

---

1. 5,000 men, not counting the women and children (Matthew 14:21).
2. *Barnes' Notes on the Old and New Testaments* (Gospel of John).

Indeed, this *"that nothing is lost"* truth was the very theme of the parables of lost things in Luke chapter 15: the Lost Sheep, the Lost Coin, and the Lost Son (the "Prodigal").

Notice the result of Jesus' instruction to His disciples to gather the remains:

> *Therefore they gathered them together, and filled twelve baskets with the fragments of the five barley loaves, which remained over and above unto them that had eaten. Then those men, when they had seen the miracle that Jesus did, said, "This is of a truth that Prophet Who should come into the world"* (John 6:13-14).

It is amazing just what remained – *"twelve baskets"* full – *"over and above."* This *"remainder"* was a vital part of the miracle! For the Scripture states that after they had gathered up the remains, *"Then ... when they had seen the miracle."*

The darkened human mind, wayward society and culture, and the influence of religious systems of this world have kept the genuine character and nature of the Father from us. The Lord Jesus Christ came to correct this by revealing the Father Himself to us. Everything about the Son of God was an unveiling of the true God. For indeed,

> *... God was in Christ, reconciling the world to Himself ...* (II Corinthians 5:19).

The Lord Jesus Christ's very words, life, death, resurrection and ascension were but a manifestation of the Father. The *"Feeding of the Five Thousand"* was no exception.

The greatest miracle of the universe is not that God has only made provision to meet the currently perceived need of salvation of mankind – now, but that all that *"remains"* at the end will be *"gathered up"* to God for His glory, so *"that NOTHING is lost."*

The salvation that we presently experience and enjoy is just the *first* part of God's great plan of redemption. We are but the "first-trusters;"[3] the "first-fruit"[4] of His

---

3. *That we should be to the praise of His glory, who **first trusted** in Chris"* (Ephesians 1:12).
4. In every harvest there is that small portion of the crop that matures early, before the vast majority of the rest. The *firstfruits* are a token of that which is to come – the full harvest. Under the Old Testament economy the *firstfruits* belonged to God, and were holy unto Him. In every generation, and in every place, God has had His *firstfruits*; those that come to harvest earlier than the rest.

full harvest. There will be no waste of any of God's creation. He created *nothing* in vain, thus ultimately none of His bounty will be squandered or lost. The *"remainder"* will be *"gathered up"* unto the Father, in His culmination of *"all things"*!

THE RECONCILIATION OF ALL THINGS

> *And, having made peace through the blood of His cross, by Him to reconcile* ALL THINGS *to Himself; by Him, I say, whether they are things in earth, or things in heaven* (Colossians 1:20).

Even though the Bible is a book specifically about the details of human redemption – Paul's unequivocal testimony is to the reconciliation of *"all things"* that have been alienated from God – not just man. To this Peter is called, by divine revelation, to confirm – *"the restitution of all things"* (Acts 13:21).

According to Paul, *"all things"* will be reconciled to God – *"all things ... in earth"* and *"all things ... in heaven."* We know what is *alienated* in the earth that needs to be reconciled to God; but what about *"in heaven"*? What is alienated there that is in need of reconciliation? Why, Satan and the fallen celestial powers, of course!

Satan[5] and the fallen celestial powers are exactly what the backdrop of Colossians 1:20 includes. Listen to Paul, just a few verses earlier – *"all things created, that are in heaven, and that are in earth, visible and invisible, whether they be thrones, or dominions, or principalities, or powers"* (:16). Again, it is clear revelation given to Paul that there will be a reconciliation of *"all things"* – all things that have been alienated. And the context is abundantly clear – the *"all things created"* ARE the *"all things"* RECONCILED.

Specifically included here in the *"all things"* are the *exact same* adversaries – the *"principalities"* and *"powers"* – against which we currently wrestle according to Ephesians 6:11-12. God says that they, too, will be reconciled. God will leave no corner of His vast and wonderful universe outside of His unfailing love.

What a blessed privilege to be the *firstfruits* of the Lord. Thus just as God has brought us to faith, so He too will bring all the rest of His creation.

> *... My wellbeloved Epaenetus, who is the firstfruits of Achaia unto Christ* (Romans 16:5).

> *Of His Own will He begot us with the Word of Truth, that we should be a kind of firstfruits of His creatures* (James 1:18).

> *... These were redeemed from among men, being the firstfruits unto God and to the Lamb* (Revelation 14:4).

5. *i.e.,* "the Adversary." The Hebrew word *"Satan,"* Strong's Hebrew Lexicon #7854, means "an opponent" and is also translated *"adversary"* in the Hebrew Scriptures. The Greek *"Satanas"* is of Chaldee origin, *Strong's Greek Lexicon* #4567, meaning "the accuser."

Therefore, the context of the reconciliation of Colossians chapter one plainly includes Satan and the fallen celestial powers. Oh, the great grace, love and mercy of God that are abundantly demonstrated and magnified in the full extent of their reach – even to the reconciliation of Satan and fallen celestial powers.

Paul repeats these gloriously triumphant truths in Ephesians 1:10.

That in the dispensation of the fulness of times He might gather together in one all things in Christ, both which are in heaven, and which are on earth; even in Him.

Again you will notice the context of *"heaven"* and *"earth."* This dual sphere is also repeated in Philippians 2:10-11:

That at the name of Jesus every knee should bow, of things in heaven, and things in earth, and things under the earth; and that every tongue should confess that Jesus Christ is Lord, to the glory of God the Father.

This reconciliation is truly *universal!* No creature will be left out. Nothing will be left alienated or unreconciled to God. There will be an entire, universal *"restoration of all things."*

For of Him, and through Him, and to Him, are all things … (Romans 11:36).

And when all things shall be subdued to Him, then shall the Son also Himself be subject to Him Who put all things under Him, that God may be All in all (I Corinthians 15:21-28).

THE OVERCOMING OF *EVIL* WITH *GOOD*

Be not overcome of evil, but overcome evil with good (Romans 12:21).

This reconciliation of *"all things"* alienated is but the disclosure and expression of the genuine nature and character of God – the overcoming of evil with good.

God's plan and purpose for His universe ultimately will be to overcome *all evil* – all of His adversaries – with good. In God's plan to *"reconcile all things unto Himself,"* He will not accomplish His work in Satan, the fallen celestial powers, and the greater part of mankind until the final judgment (the divine turning point)[6] of the *"Lake of Fire."*[7] They then will all be finally and gloriously under the righteous dominion of the Church (*ecclesia*), the Body of Christ, as we shall judge the world and angels (I Corinthians 6:1-3), with Satan under our dominion.

> *And the God of peace shall bruise Satan under your feet shortly. The grace of our Lord Jesus Christ be with you. Amen* (Romans 16:20).

This is an enlightening verse indeed. The word *"bruise"* is *Strong's Greek Lexicon* #4937, *suntribo,* which, interestingly enough, is rendered by the *King James Version* translators in Luke 4:18 as *"brokenhearted."* The word *"feet"* is *Strong's Greek Lexicon* #4228, *pous,* which is rendered by the *King James Version* translators in Matthew 5:35 as *"footstool,"* denoting dominion. Even more interesting is that *pous* is also translated right here in the book of Romans as the phrase *"are the feet of them"*:

> *... How beautiful **are the feet of them** who preach the gospel of peace, and bring glad tidings of good things!* (Romans 10:15).

---

6. The primary word translated *"judgment"* in the Greek Scriptures is *Strong's Greek Lexicon* #2920, *krisis*. This word *"krisis"* means, "a critical period of time, decisive moment, *turning point* or deciding time" (Arthur P. Adams, *Judgment*, 1885; Jack E. Jacobson, *The Concept of Circularity,* page 36), and is where we get our English word *crisis*. The *American Heritage Dictionary* defines "crisis" as "a crucial or decisive point or situation; a *turning point*." Thus *divine judgment* is the *divine crisis* in the creation. It is the divinely appointed "turning point."

7. Many see God's judgments as an end within themselves, rather than a means to an end. There are coming some wonderful days in the future, days of divine judgment, when God shall apply the refiner's fire to His creation. As in the due process of gold's and silver's refinement, these days will forever remove all the stains, disgraces and sins of the *"former things."*
Refinement's purging fire is indeed a most gracious act, producing a gloriously positive loss. It will remove all that wishes to be forgotten. As God in His forgiveness remembers them no more, so *"the former things are passed away."*
Fire is such a wonderful blessing to our daily lives. We make profitable use of it every day. The only *dangerous* fire – one that is to be feared – is a fire that is *out of control.* Be assured that the God who *"is Love"* (I John 4:8, 16), and whose love is a *"consuming fire"* (Hebrews 12:29) – is *not* out of control. As Fanny Crosby wrote in her hymn, He *"doeth all things well."*
In the Bible fire is presented as having a *purging* effect. It does so many things: it cleanses, frees, reduces, refines. It is interesting how we recognize this fact when *"fire"* is applied to the believer's judgment in I Corinthians 3:13, 15. Yet we forget this when it is applied to the unbeliever. Just as the *"fire"* of the believer's judgment is a purging, purifying act of God's love, so it is with the *"fire"* of the unbeliever's judgment.
The *"lake of fire"* is but the further manifestation of the love of God – of the love of His consuming fire – and it is defined by John as *"the second death"* (Revelation 21:8). Paul teaches us that, *"the last enemy that shall be destroyed is **death"*** (I Corinthians 15:26). That's what the *"lake of fire"* is – it is *"death."* So it shall be destroyed; and the only way to *"destroy"* death is by *"resurrection!"* The *"lake of fire"* is just the final death awaiting resurrection.

Satan will be *"brokenhearted"* under the *"footstool"* (i.e., the righteous dominion of Christ's Body) – under the *"feet of them who preach the gospel* [good news] *of peace."*

Little wonder, then, that Paul begins Romans 16:20, *"And the God of peace shall …"*

Paul did not say "And the God of *wrath* shall …" for Satan ("the Adversary") and the fallen celestial powers will no longer be aliened enemies. Having been used of God to fulfill His elementary purpose, they will be restored to the willing, humble service of thanksgiving to God. Then, because *"Satan"* will be at peace with God, his title of "Adversary" (*"Satan"*) will no longer apply.

As C.S. Lewis wrote,

> The greatest surprise for Satan will occur when he learns that he has been perfectly doing the will of God all along.

Just as God used Pharaoh in his defiance for His own purpose, so He has used Satan.

> *For the Scripture said to Pharaoh, "Even for this same purpose have I raised you up, that I might show My power in you, and that My name might be declared throughout all the earth"* (Romans 9:17).

God declared Nebuchadrezzar, the king of Babylon, to be *"My servant"* (Jeremiah 25:9), for,

> *I form the light, and create darkness: I make peace, and create evil: I the LORD do all these things* (Isaiah 45:7).

He is the grand and glorious God,

> *Who works all things after the counsel of His Own will* (Ephesians 1:11).

Do not be discouraged as you look around you. What you *see* is not the end of God's plan and purpose. Granted, the world is filled with sin and unbelief, but God is not yet done. Don't judge the final outcome by the current state of things. This is not the finished product of God.

Those of us who now trust the Lord Jesus Christ are but the beginning of God's glorious work. We are but the *first-trusters* in His glorious design. We are only the *first* part of God's great redemptive plan; there will be no waste of any of God's creation. Nothing was created by Him in vain; nothing will be squandered or lost by Him.

Ray Prinzing (1927-2005) has wonderfully written,

> The spirit of love and mercy will fully conquer all negative forces of destruction and loss, then restore *all* that which was blighted, marred, ruined; to lift the whole of creation back into harmony and peace again (*Daily Overcoming*).

God's purpose of the ages will not be complete until His full creative bounty is restored so that He is *"All in all"* (I Corinthians 15:28).

> *O the depth of the riches both of the wisdom and knowledge of God! How unsearchable are His judgments, and His ways past finding out!* (Romans 11:33).

Truly God will *"Gather up the fragments that remain, that nothing is lost"* (John 6:12).

Chapter 18

MY JOURNEY TO
Universal Reconciliation

My own journey of coming to see God's total victory over sin in His universe began in 1985 when I first embraced the distinct ministry and message of Paul. It caused me to look at everything new. I began to reevaluate everything that I have ever been taught. *Universal Reconciliation* was one of the things that came across my study path. The subject seemed so confusing to my mind, because of all that I had been taught concerning eternal conscious torment from a child. And of course, when you are busy with "the ministry" like I was at that time, trying to keep "the machine" going steady, there is little time, opportunity and encouragement to think very far "outside the box." So, for about 10 of those years I just kept this whole doctrine on "the back burner." I would "get to it" one day.

It was not until 1995, when I resigned from the pastorate, that I was really "free" (in many ways!) to seriously study the doctrine. It took me quite a long time to sort through all my baggage and through what the Bible actually taught.

What follows is a short personal narrative that catalogs the initial Scriptures that captivated my attention toward the truth that God would save all of His creation.

ROMANS 5:18

The first passage that really got my attention was Romans 5:18.

> *Therefore as by the offence of one judgment came upon all men to condemnation; even so by the righteousness of One the free gift came upon all men unto justification of life.*

I noticed that the same *"all men"* upon whom judgment came were the EXACT SAME *"all men"* upon whom the free gift came. The first was produced by Adam, the second by Jesus Christ. The result of the first was *"condemnation,"* and the result of the second was *"justification."*

I CORINTHIANS 15:22

I then saw that this was also the teaching of Paul in I Corinthians 15:22.

> *For as in Adam all die, even so in Christ shall all be made alive.*

I saw that the *"all"* who die in Adam are the EXACT SAME *"all"* who will be made alive in Jesus Christ. I realized that the passage did not say what I thought it meant, "all that are in Christ shall be made alive." I saw that it said, *"even so in Christ shall **all** be made alive."* I found my heart rejoicing! Paul was teaching that God will have the ultimate victory in winning His whole creation back to Himself.

II CORINTHIANS 5:19

Then there was Paul's contention of *world reconciliation* in II Corinthians 5:19.

> *To wit, that God was in Christ, **reconciling the world** to Himself, not imputing their trespasses to them; and has committed unto us the Word of reconciliation.*

God was in Christ, *"reconciling the world"* to Himself. I thought, could the full revelation of God's work in Christ have been made any clearer than what Paul wrote here? I could see that Paul's Gospel taught that God's plan included *all* of His creation. It was not just a potential *every-man gospel.* It is in reality *good news* for *every man.*

I was slowly beginning to realize that what Paul was teaching was that the re-demptive work of our Lord Jesus Christ was for *every* man – not potentially, but effectually.

I was seeing the great truth that Jesus Christ **"takes away** *the sin of the world"* (John 1:29). He did not make the arrangements that the sin of the world *could* be taken away. Instead, *He does it.* If it is taken away, it is no longer an issue. Paul echoes this truth.

> *To wit, that God was in Christ,* **reconciling the world to Himself, not imputing their trespasses to them;** *and has committed to us the Word of reconciliation* (II Corinthians 5:19).

I realized that the satisfaction of sin's debt was secured by Jesus Christ for *"the* **whole world."**

> *And He is the propitiation* [satisfaction] *for our sins: and not for ours only, but also for the sins of* **the whole world** (I John 2:2).

It was becoming clear to me that *"the wages of sin is death"* (Romans 6:23) and not hell as I had been taught; that death was a penalty that Christ paid for all. That was Paul's gospel, *"that Christ* **died** *for our sins"* (I Corinthians 15:6), so that *"He by the grace of God should taste death for* **every man"** (Hebrews 2:9). I had to reflect, did the Lord Jesus Christ actually *die* for **every** man? Did He actually *pay* the *penalty* for **every** man?

If what the Scriptures taught was true (and surely it is!), how could man be held responsible for a debt that has *already* been *fully paid* on his behalf? Would there not be a duplication of indebtedness if sinners were required to make a payment for sin that the Lord Jesus Christ had already made? Would there not be double jeopardy, if the sinner were held responsible? If anyone would have to pay for their own sin, then it could not be possible that our Lord actually suffered substitutionally on their account.

It was simple, He either *did* die **for** all, or He *did not* die **for** all. He was either every man's substitute, or not. If He was *every* man's substitute, then the work of redemption is obviously done and complete. If the debt was paid, and men must make their own payment, we have a double liability. God would be requiring a double payment.

SAVIOR OF THE WORLD

Whose Savior was Christ anyway? Just believers only? or the entire world's? I was seeing clearly now that He was *"the Savior of the world"* (John 4:42) – not the **"potential** Savior of the world," but was indeed, and in all actuality, *"the Savior of the world"* (John 4:42). He could not be the Savior of the World if He did not actually – in fact – save the world.

I was now realizing that Jesus Christ was, in full truth, *"the Savior of all men"* (I Timothy 4:10). Paul did not say that He was **"potentially** the Savior of all men," but that *"He is the Savior of all men."* He IS in fact their Savior. If words mean anything, He could not be their Savior if He did not save them. Yet Paul taught clearly that He is the *"Savior of all men"* because He **will** save all men.[1]

After all, Christ did not die for believers.

> *Christ died for **the ungodly*** (Romans 5:6).

> *While we were **yet sinners,** Christ died for us* (Romans 5:8).

The Lord Jesus Christ did not die for believers. He died for the ungodly, for sinners. That is indeed an every-man redemptive work!

I came to realize that I had always been taught to confuse God's current visible work with His finished product. Yet, eventually, my studies led me to the conclusion that it would only be in the ages to come that God would manifest to all creation His full plan and include them in it.

What a joy for me to see that God would not lose the majority of all His creation to sin. He would indeed redeem them all. He would have the final victory over sin!

HELL

Then, of course, there was my consideration of the subject of *hell* itself. Since Paul was God's spokesman for us today, I obviously knew I should consult his teaching when considering this important subject. I was in for a great surprise. I had never stopped to consider that Paul, our Apostle, *never once* even used the word *hell.*

---

1. The phrase, *"specially of those that believe,"* is a specialty clause. Those of us who trust Christ now, here in this life, have the added benefit of being saved from a life of emptiness, vanity, hopelessness, and despair. We are saved unto Divine life at *this present time* – a SPECIAL salvation!

He didn't use the word *hell* in any recorded messages from the Book of Acts. He didn't use the word *hell* in *any* of his epistles. Not once!

I thought, How could this possibly be? How could Paul have conducted his entire teaching ministry – one that brought glory to God – and yet never even once had used the word *hell?* Wasn't the traditional, orthodox doctrine of *hell* at the very foundation of our creeds?

How could Paul have been so negligent? How could he have gone through his entire ministry forgetting to use such a crucial word? What was up with that?

Or, was it possible that Paul understood something I didn't?

Then I considered Paul's declaration found in the Book of Acts:

> *Wherefore I take you to record this day, that I am pure from the blood of all men. For I have not shunned to declare to you **all the counsel of God*** (Acts 20:26-27).

The plain and simple fact was that Paul was *not* negligent in his teaching ministry. Here was a passage that made that clear. Paul said he was *"pure from the blood of all men,"* because he had declared *"all the counsel of God"* – a counsel which obviously *did not* include *hell* at all. Period!

Wasn't Paul presented as our present pattern (I Timothy 1:15-16)? Didn't Paul tell us to follow him (I Corinthians 4:15-17; 11:1; Philippians 3:17)?

Didn't Paul tell us to *"Hold fast the **form of sound words,** which you have **heard of me,** in faith and love which is in Christ Jesus"* (II Timothy 1:13)?

Did I hear *hell* from Paul? Was it a *Pauline* form of *sound words?*

Had I been duped into accepting a religious tradition contrary to the sound scriptural teachings of our Apostle?

Wouldn't I be Pauline if I, like Paul, also excluded *hell* from my teaching?

Or, more pointedly, could I possibly be truly Pauline in my teaching, if I continued the use of a theological system that includes the traditional *hell?*

Why would I not just follow my Apostle in teaching a pure grace gospel that had no place for, nor need of a religious *hell*?

How could Paul, the Apostle, *never* use the word hell and yet have declared *"all the counsel of God"*? How could he have been *"pure from the blood of all men"* without *ever once* using the word *hell*? I saw that I had been bewildered here because I had been steeped in the traditions of men, and not in the traditions of Paul.

> *Therefore, brothers, stand fast, and hold the traditions which you have been taught, whether by word, or our epistle* (II Thessalonians 2:15).

I was to hold Paul's traditions, *"whether by **word,** or **our epistle.**"* Holding to Paul's very words and epistles, I removed *hell* from my teaching.[2]

THE LAKE OF FIRE

Then there is the *"Lake of Fire,"* defined by the Scriptures as *"the second death."* How clear this was to me now, that the *"Lake of Fire"* is *a death – "the second death."* Yet I knew something else as well that Paul taught me: that the last enemy that God would destroy is *death.*

> *For He must reign, until He has put all enemies under His feet. The last enemy that shall be destroyed is death* (I Corinthians 15:25-26).

The last enemy that God will destroy is death. This would definitely include the *"Lake of Fire"* since it is a death – *"the second death."* The only way to *"destroy"* death is by **resurrection!**

FAITH

Don't get me wrong: I still believed that God required faith; but I had come to believe that He would bring His entire creation to that place of faith, in His *Own* good time and way.

The real question was not really whether or not some do not believe; it was simply one of timing. All would *eventually* be brought to belief by their Creator, although not all in *this* lifetime.

---

2. See chapter 3, "Paul's Teachings on Hell."

How had I made death the end of God's grace and mercy? It became clear to me that not all will be saved by pure "faith," but that it will take "sight" for some to believe.

THOMAS

Two great examples of this readily came to mind. "Doubting Thomas" was one.

The other disciples therefore said to him, "We have seen the Lord." But he said to them, "Except I shall see in His hands the print of the nails, and put my finger into the print of the nails, and thrust my hand into His side, I will not believe" (John 20:25).

To which Jesus Christ responded:

Then He said to Thomas, "Reach your finger here, and behold My hands; and reach your hand here, and thrust it into My side: and be not faithless, but believing." And Thomas answered and said to Him, "My Lord and my God." Jesus said to him, "Thomas, because you have seen Me, you have believed: blessed are they who have not seen, and yet have believed" (John 20:27-29).

Jesus said that Thomas believed by sight. *"Because you have seen Me, you have believed."* He goes on to say, *"blessed are they who have not seen, and yet have believed."*

Those of us who believe by simple faith are the firstfruit of God's full harvest. We will enjoy the First Resurrection; but this does not exclude the rest of creation, who are awaiting our manifestation (*"For the earnest expectation of the creature waits for the manifestation of the sons of God"* – Romans 8:19).

PAUL

Paul, the Apostle was another great example. Paul did not believe by simple faith. Rather, it took the "Damascus Road experience" to bring him to Christ. Both Thomas and Saul met the resurrected Christ! Oh, the extent to which God will go to reach man! He was much less limited than I was in His evangelism! He could and would pull out all the stops.

Paul says that his salvation is a pattern for those who should believe *"hereafter,"* i.e., after the close of this present dispensation. This salvation shows forth all the longsuffering of God toward the salvation of all men.

> *This is a faithful saying, and worthy of all acceptation, that Christ Jesus came into the world to save sinners; of whom I am chief. Howbeit for this cause I obtained mercy, that in me first Jesus Christ might show forth all longsuffering, for a pattern to them who should hereafter believe on Him to life everlasting. Now unto the King eternal, immortal, invisible, the only wise God, be honor and glory forever and ever. Amen* (I Timothy 1:15-17).

None in the Dispensation of Grace is saved after this "pattern" of Paul. However, *"them who should **hereafter** believe on Him"* will *see "a light from heaven, above the brightness of the sun."* They will come into the presence of the resurrected Son of God, and will with Paul call Him Lord.

> *That at the name of Jesus every knee should bow, of things in heaven, and things in earth, and things under the earth; And that every tongue should confess that Jesus Christ is Lord, to the glory of God the Father* (Philippians 2:10).

This confession that Jesus Christ is Lord can only be the work of the Holy Spirit!

> *… No man can say that Jesus is the Lord, but by the Holy Spirit* (I Corinthians 12:3).

Just reflecting on these two examples of Thomas and Paul, how can God directly intervene in the faith of some individuals, by giving them sight experience for their faith, while denying this to the multitudes? Is this fair and just, coming from a God Who is no respecter of men? Or are we missing a key ingredient in our understanding of God, of His love and His will?

I came to believe that I had misunderstood divine judgment in the Bible. I had seen it as an end, instead of a means to an end.

God is surely a God of judgment. This cannot be denied; but that is not the essence of *Who* He is.

> *God is love* (I John 4:8, 16).
> *Charity* [love] *never fails* (I Corinthians 13:8).

Love is not just one of His attributes: it *is* Him, and it never fails. More succinctly, *God* never fails! Therefore, God's judgment is *ever* subject to His love. He punishes mankind, just as a father does his children, because He loves them. Yet His punishment will be effective in bringing His creation to Himself. Divine judgment is never an end in itself, but a means to an end – and a glorious end at that!

The majority of mankind today is lost and blind; but those of us who have *first* trusted Christ (the First-trusters, Ephesians 1:12) are a part of the Firstfruits of Christ (Romans 8:23). We are but the beginning. God will reap the rest of His creation, and be *"All in all."*

LOVE AND PATIENCE

I greatly appreciate the love, concern, thoughtfulness, and patience that have been afforded me by some members of Christ's Body during my LONG transition to the *salvation of all*. Even though some have not understood, I do want each of you to know that I love you. I have not been mad, unhappy or disgruntled along this journey. I just had to be true to the Lord, and to myself, as to what I have personally come to see from my own study of the Scriptures.

FOR THOSE WHO CONCUR

I would like to add a brief word to those of you who may find yourselves in harmony with these truths. We must all remember that *"knowledge puffeth up, but charity edifieth"* (I Corinthians 8:1). Let us dare not use anything that we may learn and hold dear as a tool of division between us and other believers. May we always remember that contentious debate has its place – it belongs to the realm of the flesh – to our former identity in Adam (*c.f.* Romans 1:29; II Corinthians 12:20). We should never use any issue *against* fellow members of Christ's Body. God the Father has received all in Christ (Romans 14:3). Can we truly do any less?

> *Wherefore receive one another, as Christ has also received us to the glory of God* (Romans 15:7).

FOR THOSE WHO DON'T CONCUR

For those of you who have not yet caught a real glimpse of the *salvation of all*, I want you to know that I love you, even if you *never* agree with the conclusions of this book. We are eternally brothers!

None of what I have shared is in any way intended to pass judgment on *"another man's servant"* (Romans 14:4). Many dear and precious saints, who are effective and valuable servants for our Lord, have not embraced this teaching; yet I do not value them any less for this. I do not intend to pass my judgment or condemnation upon them.

Let every man follow the Lord out of the sincerity of his own heart, being fully persuaded in his own mind, as he enjoys the *great adventure of faith.*

> *Let every man be fully persuaded in his own mind* (Romans 14:5).

I will close with the following wonderful verses. I hope these brief thoughts will prove to be encouraging to others in their own studies.

> *And when **all things** shall be subdued to Him, then shall the Son also Himself be subject to Him Who put all things under Him, that God may be **All in all** (I Corinthians 15:28).*

> *That in the dispensation of the fulness of times He might gather together **in one all things in Christ,** both which are in heaven, and which are on earth; even in Him (Ephesians 1:10).*

> *And, having made peace through the blood of His cross, by Him **to reconcile all things to Himself;** by Him, I say, whether they are things in earth, or things in heaven (Colossians 1:20).*

Therefore as by the offense of one judgment came upon all men to condemnation; even so by the righteousness of One the free gift came upon all men to justification of life. For as by one man's disobedience many were made sinners, so by the obedience of One shall many be made righteous.

~ Romans 5:18-19

Chapter 19

THE "MANY" AND THE "ALL"

Some are confused by passages of Scripture which carry both "many" with "all" in its context dealing with the salvation of all. This selection from Romans 5:18-19 is an example.

In this passage the word "many" does not exclude all. The word "many" does not exclude all, except specifically by context. Context always determines word meanings.

Example:

There were *many* people at the ballgame.

So, how *many* were at the ballgame? All were.

The "many" is a reference to a quantity – a large quantity, and in this example it includes *everyone* at the ballgame. In this case the word "many" refers to "all," and no one is excluded.

Another Example:

There were many people who spoke Spanish at the ballgame.

In this case we have limited the quantity of the "many" by the context. The "many" now are not the entire size of the crowd attending the game, but the size of those speaking Spanish at the event.

We see in Romans 5:18 that the effect of Adam's offense, as well as Christ's righteousness, was on *ALL.*

In :19 we see how large the "ALL" group is – they are "MANY" affected by the actions of the two men.

The "all" in :18 describes the effects to be without the exception of anyone. The "many" of :19 describes the MASSIVENESS of the effect – the "all" were not just a "few" (small in quantity), but "many" (large in quantity.)

Romans 5:19 says, *"For by one man's disobedience MANY were made sinners."* How many were affected by Adam's disobedience? ALL! (We know this from the "all" in :18.) The "all" was a MASSIVE group, as shown by the use of the word "many"!

Romans 5:19 also says, *"so by the obedience of one shall many be made righteous."* How many were affected by Christ's obedience? *ALL!* (We know this also from the "all" in :18.) The "all" was the same MASSIVE group, as shown by the use of the word "many"!

In Romans 5:18, the exact same "all" who were *condemned* in Adam's offense were the exact same "all" who were *justified* in Christ's obedience.

In Romans 5:19, the exact same "many" who were *made sinners* in Adam's disobedience were the exact same "many" who were *made righteous* in Christ's obedience.

Let's say that the ballgame we mentioned earlier was a professional football game; and only 100 people were in attendance.

"All at the game wore red jerseys." This means that everyone at the game wore a red jersey. None would be excluded in this "all" – but this "all" would NOT be "many" since only 100 people were there. As stated earlier, "many" is defined by its context. So, in this example the "all" would not be "many," because 100 people at an 80,000 seat NFL stadium would never be referred to as "many." The "all" would be only a "few."

Now if the stadium was FULL of people, and everyone without a single exception wore red jerseys, then it could be said that "all" wore red jerseys, and that there were "many" red jerseys there. The "many" and the "all" would be the same in the context. So it is with Paul's teaching in Romans 5:18-19.

The "many" and "all" can also be seen in other similar "salvation of all" passages. Be on the lookout for them.

Note to Appendices

The following appendices are quotes that have been gleaned from the writings of various authors. A few of the authors do not hold the doctrine of the *Salvation of All*, but I have found their comments enlightening as they relate to the subject.

Appendix 1

I Will Draw All Men to Me

"And I, if I be lifted up from the earth, will draw all men unto Me" (John 12:32).

Therefore, if *"all men"* are to be drawn to Him, His words await their perfect fulfillment. The present age of grace does not exhaust the possibilities of His power, for, as the grand Executor of God's will, glorious work awaits the Son of God in ages yet unrolled.

Remembering, too, that God, as the Savior of all men (I Timothy 4:9-11), wills all humanity to be saved (I Timothy 2:4) by virtue of Christ's kingly ransom for all (I Timothy 2:6), we should glory in redemption so amazingly complete.

We see then, that He who fashioned and formed, can perfect and complete. All the marvelous details of His will move with stately strides toward His desired conclusion. He is the God of patience, even as He is the God of hope.

In thinking of such vastness of grace, we must distinguish between the immediate and the ultimate, between development and completion.

Now is the fragmentary, then the complete. His way is perfect, His will supreme. May it be ours to wait patiently for Him, that your hearts and intellects will rest in His ability to bring to glad fulfillment the operations of His majestic will.

William Mealand (1873-1957)
Unsearchable Riches
(Volume 9, 1917)

Appendix 2

THE CENTER OF THE BOOK OF ROMANS

"Therefore as by the offence of one judgment came upon all men to condemnation; even so by the righteousness of one the free gift came upon all men unto justification of life. For as by one man's disobedience many were made sinners, so by the obedience of one shall many be made righteous" (Romans 5:18-19).

As mankind's connection with Adam involved him in certain death, through sin, so his relation to Christ insures to him *life without fail*. Thus these verses give us the logical center of the epistle. They are the very central point to which everything that precedes converges, and out of which everything that follows will flow.

The great ideas of sin, death and judgment are here shown to be involved in the connection of the human race with Adam, but over against this we have the blessed fact of a union with Christ, and in this union, righteousness and life. This double headship of mankind in Adam and Christ shows the significance of the work of redemption for *the entire race*.

Up to the present point the Apostle has been dealing with *sins*, as they are expressed in human life but now he proceeds to deal with *sin*, the principle from which all expressions proceed. He thus goes to the root of the trouble -- sin, and shows the disease and its remedy. Although he has clearly proved our justification from *sins*, there still remains the question of the old nature, and now he is about to show how we obtain deliverance from *SIN* as well as from *sins.*

He ranges mankind under two heads -- Adam and Christ. There are two men, two acts, and two results. In this profound teaching we have the spiritual and theological illustrations of the great modern principle of solidarity. The latter solidarity far surpasses the former in the quality of the obedience of Christ as compared with Adam, and in the effects of the work of Christ for justification and life. It will be seen that the purpose of the section is not to *teach* sin, but assuming it as a fact, to *show* how divine grace *overcomes it in "ALL"* (Romans 5:18) …

If *the* "many" were involved in sin and death through the agency of the one man Adam, "much more" may we believe that *the* "many" will be involved in righteousness and life through the agency of the One Man, Christ Jesus …

Adam's one offense brought judgment to all men to their condemnation. None escape this condemnation to death. *"For as in Adam all die, EVEN SO,"* Christ's one act of righteousness brings the free gift unto all men to their justification of life. Not one will be left out. *"In Christ shall all be made alive."* (I Corinthians 15:22).

W.H. Griffith Thomas (1861-1924)
The Presbyterian
June 1932

Appendix 3

ALL THINGS ARE OF GOD

"And all things are of God..." (II Corinthians 5:18).

There is no statement in the Bible, that was made by an apostle, that is more remarkable and even startling than this statement. When you think of it seriously, it seems as though Paul was very unguarded and careless in his language. We are apt to think that he ought to have modified and limited it in some way, such as for instance, all *good* things are of God.

But no, Paul makes the sweeping, unqualified statement, *"All things are of [i.e., out of] God."* Furthermore, so important did Paul consider this truth that he repeats it over and over again. The direct statement is made no less than six times in the writings of the apostle:

"For of Him, and through Him, and to Him, are all things: to Whom be glory for ever. Amen." (Romans 11:36).

"But to us there is but one God, the Father, of Whom are all things, and we in Him; and one Lord Jesus Christ, by Whom are all things, and we by Him" (I Corinthians 8:6).

"For as the woman is of the man, even so is the man also by the woman; but all things of God" (I Corinthians 11:12).

"And all things are of God, Who hath reconciled us to Himself by Jesus Christ, and hath given to us the ministry of reconciliation" (II Corinthians 5:18).

"In Whom also we have obtained an inheritance, being predestinated according to the purpose of Him who worketh all things after the counsel of His own will" (Ephesians 1:11).

"For it became Him, for Whom are all things, and by Whom are all things, in bringing many sons unto glory, to make the Captain of their salvation perfect through sufferings" (Hebrews 2:10).

Now, was the apostle careless and a little too bold in these utterances, or did he mean just what he said, and are they true, taken full strength? I say, without any hesitation, yes, to the two latter questions. The more we learn (the more revelation) of God's works and ways the more we shall understand that in a sense absolutely *"all things are of God."*

Arthur P. Adams
Beverly, MA
1885

Appendix 4

RECONCILIATION OF THE WORLD
This *Is* the Gospel!

"To wit, that God was in Christ, reconciling the world unto Himself, not imputing their trespasses unto them; and hath committed unto us the word of reconciliation" (II Corinthians 5:19).

The failure or refusal to discern the Pauline Gospel as a separate and new revelation and not a "development from Judaism," accounts for two-thirds of the confusion in many people's minds today as regards just what the Gospel is. Paul's Gospel will suffer no admixture with works on the one hand or religious pretensions and performances on the other. It is as simple and clear as the sunlight from heaven. The end of *man* is where God *begins* in Romans 3, at what might be called the opening of the Pauline Revelation. Most unsaved people today believe in their hearts that the reason they are not saved is because of something they have not yet done, some step that remains for them to take before God will accept them. But this is *absolutely untrue.* When Christ said, *"It is finished,"* He meant that He had, then and there, paid the debt for the *whole* human race. *"He gave Himself a ransom for all"* (I Timothy 2:6).

Now, Paul, in his wonderful revelation declares that God hath reconciled the world to Himself; that *"God was in Christ* [at the cross] *reconciling the world unto Himself"* (II Corinthians 5:19). Men do not know this, but they conceive that something stands between them and God, before God will accept or forgive them. If you tell a man that God is demanding no good works of him whatsoever, no religious observance or church ordinances, that God is not asking him to undertake any duties at all, but that God invites him to believe a glad message that his sins have already been dealt with at the Cross, and that God expects him to believe it – if you tell an unsaved man such a story as this, he is astonished and overwhelmed – yet this *is* the Gospel!

William R. Newell (1868-1956)
Paul's Gospel

Appendix 5

GOD'S WRATH

What is translated as *"wrath"* in conventional translations cannot – as commonly believed – be an essential change of disposition on God's part toward man. God has only one disposition, one inclination, one divine posture in His relationship with man, that of unconditional love coming to us in unearned grace. He is determined to fully give Himself to us unreservedly. When one sees this, we become His bond slave, bound by such love.

The primary Greek work translated as "wrath"[1] is *orge,* from which we get our English word, "orgy," and it's various forms. The word itself and it's root conveys aroused passion, excitement, a reaching after and overlaps in meaning with *thumos,* translated also as *"wrath."* Ed Browne, translates *orge* as (God's) "intrinsic fervor." I like that. I think Ed has captured the essential meaning. For me, it suggests ravishing love.

Since God *is* love, then wrath necessarily is a form of love, for nothing could proceed out from the nature of God that is inconsistent with the love that He IS. The conclusion is just too obvious once one has been delivered from the dark, demonic imagination that fuels eternal torment dogma; namely, that God,

---

1. James Strong: Greek #3709 "Desire", "Excitement of the mind."
   W.E. Vine: "Originially any natural impulse or desire, or disposition."
   E.W. Bullinger: "The mind, the spirit that is breathed out, an intense passion of the mind."
   J.H. Thayer: "To teem, denoting an internal motion, especially that of plants and fruits swelling with juice."

when faced with the ontological contrarianism that seeks to impose on us a false identity, with us being overcome by a false persona, His love is aroused to reclaim us, to lay claim with divine jealousy to that which belongs to Him. With intrinsic fervor He reaches out to possess that which is His, and we are His by creation and by redemption …

What is commonly called *"the wrath of God,"* is that quality of love that will not let us go, and will not let us miss the glory of His love. It's an awesome, passionate, jealous, intense, possessive love, that when heated up fills us with awe. Initially it can be terribly frightening to be the object of such fervor.

I think of the old song about Casey waltzing with the strawberry blond. "His brain was so loaded it nearly exploded, the poor girl would shake with alarm …"

Whenever we are not participating in the faith of Christ, when we are not ongoingly believing in Christ, sharing His restful trust in the Father's perfect love, His intrinsic fervor abides on us. He becomes, out from the depths of His love, a consuming fire, utterly radical in His pursuit of us, even to the cross.

John R. Gavazzoni
The Cup of God's Wrath
2006

Appendix 6

BLESSINGS OF GOD UPON SODOM

*"… When your sisters, Sodom and her daughters, **shall return to their former estate**, and Samaria and her daughters shall return to their former estate …"* (Ezekiel 16:55).

Many people are not aware that the Bible declares that Sodom and Gomorrah shall be raised up again in the day of judgment to be corrected and finally restored to their former estate. What a merciful and loving God! …

As far as the destruction of the city is concerned, it was necessary, and part of the purpose of God to bring about His progressive revelation in the earth. But we must keep in mind that just because God pours out judgment and wrath on people, does not mean that He has cast them off forever. His judgments and His wrath do not last forever. They are temporary and for the purpose of correction. Oh that Christians would be able to understand this about their Heavenly Father! God does not condone wickedness of any kind. But God is able to correct the sinner and restore him to his former estate. Remember … God is Love! Remember … Love never fails! It is impossible for God to give up on Sodom and Gomorrah, for He loves them, and His love will never fail them!

Isaiah 57:16 states,

"… For I [God] will not contend for ever, neither will I be always wroth …"

Lamentations 3:31-32 states,

> *"... For the Lord will not cast off for ever: But though He cause grief, yet will He have compassion according to the multitudes of His mercies ..."*

Let God show you His great compassion and mercy for all.

God loves all, even Sodom and Gomorrah!

Thomas Kissinger
The Glory of God and the Honor of Kings
Devotion for February 4

Appendix 7

CONTRASTS BETWEEN UNIVERSAL STATEMENTS

"Therefore as by the offence of one judgment came upon all men to condemnation; even so by the righteousness of one the free gift came upon all men unto justification of life" (Romans 5:18).

"For God hath concluded them all in unbelief, that he might have mercy upon all" (Romans 11:32).

"For as in Adam all die, even so in Christ shall all be made alive" (I Corinthians 15:22).

In each of these texts, we encounter a contrast between two universal statements, and in each case the first "all" seems to determine the scope of the second. Accordingly, when Paul asserts in Romans 5:18 that Christ's one act of righteousness leads to justification and life for all, he evidently has in mind every descendant of Adam who stands under the judgment of condemnation; when he insists in Romans 11:32 that God is merciful to all, he has in mind every human being who God has "shut up" to, or has "imprisoned" in, disobedience; and finally, when he asserts in I Corinthians 15:22 that "all shall be made alive" in Christ, he has in mind everyone who has died in Adam. The grammatical evidence here seems utterly decisive; you can reject it only if you are prepared to reject what is right before your eyes.

Thomas Talbott
The Inescapable Love of God
1999, Pages 59, 60

Appendix 8

ABRAHAM LINCOLN AND THE SALVATION OF ALL

Independent Testimonies of Abraham Lincoln's Belief in the *Salvation of All*

Occasionally over the years, my study of *Universal Reconciliation* has led me to the man, Abraham Lincoln. As our country celebrates the bicentennial of his birth, I thought it might be appropriate to share some of the resources I have found regarding his belief in the *salvation of all*.

Many do not know that for almost all of Abraham Lincoln's life he held a firm conviction that I Corinthians 15:22 was the bedrock of Christ's redemptive work. He found great hope, expounding upon its theme.

What follows is a list of five independent testimonies spanning a period of thirty years of Abraham Lincoln's life, witnessing to his belief that *all men* would ultimately be saved through the redemptive work of the Lord Jesus Christ.

Mentor Graham's Testimony

Mentor Graham (1800-1886) was an early schoolmaster of Abraham Lincoln who eventually became intimate friends with him. Lincoln boarded with him for two years. In later years he assisted Lincoln in his speech writing.

Abraham Lincoln was living at my house at New Salem, going to school, studying English grammar and surveying, in the year 1833. One morning he said to me, "Graham, what do you think about the anger of the Lord?" I replied, "I believe the Lord never was angry or mad and never would be; that His loving-kindness endureth forever; that He never changes." Said Lincoln, "I have a little manuscript written, which I will show you," and stated he thought of having it published. The size of the manuscript was about one half quire of foolscap, written in a very plain hand, on the subject of Christianity, and a defense of universal salvation. The commencement of it was something respecting the God of the universe never being excited, mad or angry. I had the manuscript in my possession some week or ten days. I have read many books on the subject of theology, and I don't think, in point of perspicuity and plainness of reasoning, I ever read one to surpass it. I remember well his argument. He took the passage, *"As in Adam all die, even so in Christ shall all be made alive,"* and followed up with the proposition that whatever the breach or injury of Adam's transgressions to the human race was, which no doubt was very great, was made just and right by the atonement of Christ.[1]

Erasmus Manford's Testimony

Erasmus Manford (1815-1884) was a capable Bible teacher, author and publisher, who taught *the salvation of all*. His periodicals had extensive circulations.[2] He is best known for his 1849 work, *150 Reasons for Believing in the Final Salvation of All Mankind*. Abraham Lincoln was one of his supporters, himself attending his lectures.

In Manford's autobiography he recounts Lincoln's attendance to one of his addresses on universal reconciliation:

I remember well seeing Mr. Lincoln then punctually every day and night. He often nodded his head to me when I made a strong point.[3]

---

1. A signed letter of Mentor Graham, published by William Eleazar Barton in The Soul of Abraham Lincoln, Barton, (1920) pp. 346-347.
2. Among his periodicals: Christian Teacher, Golden Era, Manford's Monthly Magazine, Western Universalist.
3. Twenty-five Years in the West, Erasmus Manford (1867), p. 219.

Jonathan Harnett's Testimony

Jonathan Harnett was a Lincoln associate and business man from Pleasant Plains, IL.

Harnett retold of his 1858 conversation with Lincoln and some of their associates:

> … closed with the restitution of all things to God, as the doctrine taught in the Scriptures, and if anyone was left in doubt in regard to his belief in the atonement of Christ and the final salvation of all men, he removed those doubts in a few questions he answered and propounded to others. After expressing himself, some one or two took exceptions to his position, and he asked a few questions that cornered his interrogators and left no room to doubt or question his soundness on the atonement of Christ, and salvation finally of all men. He did not pretend to know just when that event would be consummated, but that it would be the ultimate result, that Christ must reign supreme, high over all. The Savior of all; and the supreme Ruler, he could not be with one out of the fold; all must come in, with his understanding of the doctrine taught in the Scriptures.[4]

Isaac Cogdal's Testimony

Isaac Cogdal was a longtime friend of Lincoln, who recounts his 1859 conversation with Lincoln.

> Lincoln expressed himself … He did not nor could not believe in the endless punishment of any one of the human race. He understood punishment for sin to be a Bible doctrine; that the punishment was parental in its object, aim, and design, and intended for the good of the offender; hence it must cease when justice is satisfied. He added that all that was lost by the transgression of Adam was made good by the atonement: all that was lost by the fall was made good by the sacrifice.[5]

James Shrigley's Testimony

James Shrigley (1813-1905) was a Universalist minister, U.S. Army chaplain, historian and author. He served churches in: Exeter, New Hampshire, 1838-39;

---

4. William J. Wolf, *The Almost Chosen People,* Doubleday & Company Inc, 1959, pp. 105-106.
5. *Ibid.,* p. 104.

Baltimore, Maryland, 1841-48; Reading, Pennsylvania, 1850-54 and 1856-58; Philadelphia, Pennsylvania, 1854-56; and Richmond, Virginia, 1858-61.

During the Civil War, Shrigley was appointed by Abraham Lincoln as a United States Army chaplain. A group of Protestant ministers traveled to Washington hoping to dissuade President Abraham Lincoln from making the appointment. The President asked on what grounds they were opposed to Shrigley. They replied that Shrigley believed in the salvation of all souls, and that even the rebels would be saved! Lincoln's response was that, if that be so, then Shrigley deserved to be a Chaplain in the U.S. Army.[6]

6. Nelson C. Simonson, *Dictionary of Unitarian & Universalist Biography,* Unitarian Universalist Historical Society.

Appendix 9

Universalism an Utterance of the Heart

Introduce the topic of universalism, and many Christians will point out instantly that it contradicts Holy Scripture. And when one peruses its pages, it may appear so. But one thing is undeniable by anyone whose heart goes out to others: We intuitively hope universalism is true.

Their kind-hearted and merciful wish is that God might finally bring all humanity into the circle of His grace. If they could, they would decree the redemption of every person on the planet. They would see the ultimate reform of each sinner, were the choice theirs.

And yet, the love, mercy and compassion of such souls falls far below God's. The span between heaven and earth is the span between our love and His. Man's mercy falters; God's mercy "endures forever." (I Chronicles 16:34) Man's love wears thin; God, on the other hand, IS love. (I John 4:8). Man's compassion extends just so far; God has compassion "over all His works" (Psalm 145:9).

That being the case, how can we assert that God will save fewer – much, much fewer, in fact – than the finite mercy of man would save? Does perfect love redeem a smaller company than would imperfect love?

Many at this point flee for refuge to the inscrutable ways of God. The Lord's thoughts are not our thoughts, they remind us. He does not always act according to His creatures' logic. This is true, of course.

But the common rebuttal leaves us with a baffling incongruity. Consider the tendency of humanity: The less godly a man, the narrower his mercy and love. The godlier a man, the broader, the more liberal his. Then consider God, the one whose character the godly emulate. Inexplicably, when love and mercy reach the zenith of perfection, the trend appears to reverse itself. The scope of redemptive mercy constricts. Most of his creatures cease being objects of mercy and become objects of wrath instead.

Isn't there something wrong with this theological picture? Flawed mercy would rescue all. Impeccable mercy will not. In light of such an enigma, we can't help but ask: Could it be that the larger portion of the Christian tradition has missed the mark on this subject?

Some will argue that although God wishes to restore all people, He will not violate our free will. How this free will becomes so invincible, so able to wear down omnipotence, remains to be explained. And why God's action against it would be a "violation" – as if He is subject to a higher law than Himself – is also unanswerable.

God is able to remove the heart of stone and replace it with a heart of flesh. He can work in us to will and to do according to His good pleasure. What human father would hesitate to "violate" the free will of a son who suddenly chooses to dash toward traffic? God is the parent of us all (Malachi 2:10).[1] We are His offspring (Acts 17:28).[2] Would He then not do everything in His power – a power that knows no bounds – to lead us away from ultimate destruction?

There is something intuitive about our desire to expand redemption beyond orthodox boundaries. This is significant. In the first chapter of Romans, Paul expresses a belief that all humans have a law written on the heart. They have an inner monitor that informs them of such concepts as love, mercy, equity. Could it be that this principle is at war with the words of theologians and preachers? Might this explain the unrest of so many? …

Steve Jones
(Former Pastor)

Appendix 10

WHAT IF SOME DO NOT BELIEVE?

The Apostle Paul asks the question,

"For what if some did not believe? shall their unbelief make the faith of God without effect? God forbid." (Romans 3:3).

"If we believe not, yet He abideth faithful: He cannot deny Himself" (II Timothy 2:13).

It should always be kept in mind, that a thing must be true before it is a subject of belief, and if so, belief of, or unbelieving, cannot effect the thing itself.

For example, one might believe at night that the sun would never appear again – nay, the whole world might believe it, and while this would have a very important influence upon the people themselves, it would in no wise prevent the sun's coming forth again in beauty and glory.

So, in relation to God's promises relating to man's final destiny – the belief or disbelief of them cannot affect the truth itself. God cannot deny himself – He is faithful and true and the plain difference is while the believer enters into rest, rejoices with joy unspeakable and full of glory, the unbeliever is in darkness, doubt and gloom, shut out from the light and glory of the Gospel of peace and love.

Herein lies one great error of common religionists – they suppose that if they believe that Christ is their Savior, He is their Savior – otherwise that He is not so. Well, if He is not the Savior of unbelievers, the unbeliever is called upon to believe a lie in order to be saved. Jesus certainly died to save all before any believed on Him, and all the promises of future redemption were given while almost the entire world was lying in wickedness.

God is the Savior of all men in the sense of eternal salvation in the future world, whether they believe it or not, and those who heed the promise of his grace are privileged to look forward with fair prospects to the spirit land, and take hold of the joys of heaven by anticipation.

> *"He that believeth on the Son of God hath the witness in himself; he that believeth not God hath made him a liar; because he believeth not the record that God gave of His Son. And this is the record that God hath given to us, eternal life, and this life is in His Son"* (I John 5:10-11).

Now can any one suppose that if all had not eternal life in Christ the disbelief of the fact would make God a liar? If it were not then, any man who said it was not, would only tell the plain truth. But being true, by promise, independent of human belief, faith gives to each one the witness in himself that the gift will be received at the proper time. It belongs to us to believe with all the heart – to stagger not at the promises of God, and to enter into that rest which can be found no where else.

S. J. M.
Universalist Herald and Progressionist
October 7, 1859

Appendix 11

GOD IN REDEMPTION

"Therefore as by the offence of one judgment came upon all men to condemnation; even so by the righteousness of one the free gift came upon all men unto justification of life. For as by one man's disobedience many were made sinners, so by the obedience of one shall many be made righteous. Moreover the law entered, that the offence might abound. But where sin abounded, grace did much more abound: That as sin hath reigned unto death, even so might grace reign through righteousness unto eternal life by Jesus Christ our Lord" (Romans 5:18-21).

The closing verses of Romans 5 have been the standing perplexity of theologians. Yet nowhere has the Holy Spirit written for our learning plainer conclusions, and never has tradition been blinder than in the treatment of this magnificent passage. Believe the passage as it stands, and the divine logic is irresistible.

It contains a comparison between the first and the last Adam. What the first Adam was, and is, to the whole human race, the last Adam is, and will be also, to the whole human race.

"Therefore as by the offence of one judgment came upon all men to condemnation; even so by the righteousness of one the free gift came upon all men unto justification of life" (Romans 5:18).

There follows a reiteration of the comparison with its Divine logic, so that the fact might be stated again, not only as a climax in the purpose of redemption, but as a future goal in the history of the working out of the redemption of all men.

> *"For as by one man's disobedience many were made sinners, so by the obedience of one shall many be made righteous"* (Romans 5:19).

The company of the righteous is identical in person and number with the company of the sinners to which the passage refers.

So that we have two phrases in these two verses, by which we can establish beyond question the identity of those under discussion. These two phrases are *"all men,"* and the *"many."* Of this company it is declared in the first place, that *"all men"* and the *"many"* were made sinners and come into condemnation; and in the second place, that *"all men"* and the *"many"* will be made righteous, not simply saved but made righteous.

If this plain simple language – and God could not have made it plainer – does not mean what it says, but infers something quite the opposite, so that the comparison used is not a true one, then we may well pause to ask how ever it came about that on such a subject, and at such a climax in his argument, Paul did not tell us exactly what he meant.

If he meant that all men would be influenced by Adam's sin hopelessly and completely, but only some of the race would be affected actually by Christ's cross, here was the place to make this difference once and for all clear. Instead, however, he uses universal terms, and logical comparisons, which, if the last suggestion is true, are not only bewildering but positively untrue, without the faintest hint to the contrary.

The apostle does more than this. He introduces a vivid contrast.

> *"But **not as** the offence, **so also** is the free gift. For if through the offence of one many be dead, much more the grace of God, and the gift by grace, which is by one man, Jesus Christ, hath abounded unto many"* (Romans 5:15).

Let the reader note that the contrast here is in an absolutely opposite direction to the conclusions of ordinary theology. Most of us were taught that there was such a contrast between the effect of Adam's sin and Christ's righteousness that by the fall all were lost, and by the Cross some would be saved. The contrast here in verse 15 is the direct opposite of this conclusion. It is between the effect of the acts of the two Adams, and is such a contrast that the grace of God hath "***much more ... abounded***" in the Cross over the act of the first Adam.

If a human act was effectual for ruin, how much more shall a Divine act be effectual for salvation? The Apostle repeats this contrast later in the closing verse of the argument, when he sums up with the words, *"where sin abounded grace did **much more abound**."*

It is incomprehensible that such reckless language would have been chosen, if the Apostle did not mean just what the words declare; especially in the entire absence of any modifying or cautionary phrases.

The compound word here implies, "not only abounding," that is, bursting forth round about; round about all ages, round about all nations, round about all sorts: but "superabounding" – that surrounding all those rounds, and with surplus and advantage over-flowing all: not only abounding grace, abounding unto all, to the whole world, but grace superabounding: that is, if there were other worlds, grace would bring salvation even unto them. (Dr. Clarke).

The argument reveals the principle upon which God is working out His purpose with the human race. It declares that the principle upon which God is working to the redemption of all is the same principle by which the universal fall of man came about. Through one man's sin the whole race was involved surely and hopelessly. Adam's offence did not merely make it possible for men to sin and merit condemnation, it made it *impossible* for them to do otherwise.

Through another Man's righteousness therefore, even the Man of Calvary, the human race was saved, as through Adam it was lost. And as all men, born or yet unborn, will not escape the contamination and condemnation of that act of sin in Eden, so to all men there will eventually come the blessed results of that act upon Calvary.

When we catch the thought of the two federal headships, the logical issue is so clear that the statement of the fact of redemption being co-extensive with the fall in its reach and results is so evident in the passage that faith leaps to appropriate the truth.

The subject of the federal headship of Adam and Christ has been put so clearly by D.M. Panton that we cannot do better than quote at length from his pen:

> So the Holy Ghost says: '*By one man*' – the fountain of human blood; the sample man, because no man can deny that he too would have acted exactly as Adam did – '*sin entered into the world, and death by sin;*' entered, for both sin and death are for ever aliens in the universe of God; and so death passed unto all men '*for that all have sinned*' (Romans 5:12) in Eden.

> When God made Adam He made all men; for the race is no aggregate of isolated and independent units, but an entity of organic and dependent generations: and, since God made of '*one blood*' all the nations of men, sin introduced anywhere is sin introduced everywhere. The fall of Adam was the fall of souls at this moment not yet born; and the fact of their sinning, when born, will for ever prove the truth of the doctrine.

> Upon this organic fall of all in the one God builds the whole structure of redemption; for He takes this very principle of solidarity, which was our ruin, and makes that solidarity the organ of the world's salvation. '*For as by one man's disobedience many were made sinners*' – sinners by a representative act, sinners by a fouled nature inherited, sinners ourselves by active choice – '***even so***' – God taking the solidarity which ruined as the solidarity which shall redeem – '*by the obedience of the One shall many be made righteous.*'

> The helpless fall of the race into death through the act of a lonely man is countered by a helpless salvation for the entire race wrought by a Man as lonely and unique. That is, God incarnate in human flesh, the Second Man, is so organically one with the race as a race – so the Son of man, not a son of man – that His righteousness is imputed to all as actually and as really as is Adam's sin. The first Adam was the federal head of the race; the last Adam is equally the federal head of the race; the first Adam, the law-breaker, is replaced by the last Adam, the law-fulfiller: the first man acted for all mankind, and plunged the world into ruin; the Second Man acted for all mankind, and lifted the World into salvation: Adam was the author of death to all: Christ is the author of life for all.

> The Holy Ghost says: '*by the offence of one*' – for however often Adam sinned afterwards, we fell only by one act that introduced sin itself – '*judgment came upon all men to condemnation;* ***even so***' – God turning solidarity, the organ

of condemnation, into solidarity, the organ of grace – '*by the righteousness of one the free gift came upon all men unto justification of life.*' As Adam ruined us through sin foreign to us, without our fault; so Christ has saved us with righteousness foreign to us, without our merit: and the Holy Spirit thus rests our entire redemption on the historical, actual, personal fall of the first man countered by the historical, actual, personal death and resurrection of the Second Man.

So, as one man condemns all, the Other justifies all; and both these acts are completely finished in Adam and Christ ... As we were lost in Adam six thousand years before we were born, so we were saved by Christ two thousand years before our birth. We are as helpless in our salvation as we were in our fall.

The difficulties in the way of the acceptance of the literal interpretation of this passage owe their existence to the following reasons, amongst others:

1. The innate tendency of the human mind to choose the lesser ideal of God.

Instead of modifying the negative passages by those that affirm a redemption co-extensive with the fall, the human mind has persistently preferred the opposite method, and modified this great passage. The first thing to be removed, before the altered perspective of the Divine ultimate is accepted is this tendency to gauge God by His attributes of justice and righteousness, rather than by His nature which is Love. The former are not sacrificed to the latter, but are means by which love realizes its goal.

2. The confusion of the process of salvation with the goal.

All the dread warnings and threatened judgments of the New Testament have to do with the process by which the goal is reached. The administration of redemption is in the hands of the Son of God. Into His hands the Father has delivered all things (John 3:35). The failure to see this has resulted in those activities of Christ, as Judge of mankind, being projected into eternity, instead of being kept within the bounds of His kingdom, which is strictly in time and will be delivered up to the Father at the end of time.

3. The confusion of the special salvation of this age with the general salvation of all men, to which God equally pledges Himself in His Word.

"He is the Savior of the Body" (Ephesians 5:23). He is also the *"the Savior of the world"* (John 4:42, I John 4:14, I Timothy 4:10). These two distinct functions were present to the Lord's own mind when He affirmed the certainty that *"All that the Father giveth Me* **shall come to Me,"** and with equal certainty declared that *"I, if I be lifted up from the earth* **will draw all men unto Me."**

That first company are being thus drawn by wondrous ways of grace from all classes and out of all conditions of men under circumstances that reveal the sovereignty of God that lies back of their salvation, the Saviour deliberately limited to the Father's will and choice. *"No man can come unto Me except the Father which hath sent Me draw him."*

It was given to Paul in particular to unfold in his epistles this twin truth. He boldly declares that in the dispensation of the fullness of times God will gather together in one all things in Christ, and that we in this age who have **"first** trusted in Christ," have by sovereign grace been *"predestinated according to the purpose of Him who worketh all things after the counsel of His own will"* (Ephesians 1:9-12).

The same double issue of the Cross is again presented in the Colossian epistle. The definite undertaking to fully reconcile all things eventually by means of that Cross, is given side by side with the earnest of it in the actual reconciliation of the believers of this age.

> *"And, having made peace through the blood of His cross, by Him to reconcile all things unto Himself; by Him, I say, whether they be things in earth, or things in heaven. And you, that were sometime alienated and enemies in your mind by wicked works, yet* **now** *hath He reconciled"* (Colossians 1:20-21).

As this was the inspiration of the Savior's ministry, so it was of Paul's, who rejoiced that the living God was *"the Saviour of all men, specially of those that believe"* (I Timothy 4:10); and who therefore bent his energies to the accomplishment of the first out-working of salvation, and endured all things for the elects' sake that they might also obtain the salvation which is in Christ Jesus with eternal glory – that special salvation which carries with it the glories of the ages to come, in which the administration of redemption, by means of judgment and grace, goes on apace under the ministry of Christ and His church.

How sadly man has misunderstood this dual purpose and dragged the glorious doctrine of election into the dust, is manifest in the distorted view of predestination presented by the popular theology of the day. Basing everything upon one sentence – wrung from one passage, with utter disregard for context, kindred passages, translation, or the words of Christ to the contrary – we are told that predestination simply means that God foreknew who would believe and predestinated such for salvation! This is contrary to every other utterance of God on this great subject. *"Ye have not chosen Me but I have chosen you"* was Christ's explanation of the matter, and Paul emphatically declares that election was prior to, and independent of, the actions of the sample case he gives of Jacob and Esau,

> *"(For the children being not yet born, neither having done any good or evil, that the purpose of God according to election might stand, not of works, but of Him that calleth;) It was said unto her, The elder shall serve the younger"* (Romans 9:11).

The summing up of the Apostle's argument on this very point is,

> *"So then it is not of him that willeth, nor of him that runneth, but of God that sheweth mercy"* (Romans 9:16).

All is based upon God's *"good, and acceptable, and perfect will."* Man would invert the order and base all upon the fickle will of man, enslaved by sin (John 8:34). Having mistaken the present purpose of God in this age so hopelessly it is little wonder the larger issue is obscured altogether.

The distortion is due to the effort to explain away the apparent favoritism of God for some, with his apparent rejection of others, and to square the doctrine of election with the fundamental principle in God's dealing with men that He is no respecter of persons. Thus grace is turned into works, and faith, the gift of God, becomes the minimum of man's effort that saves him. How far removed is this conception of the Gospel, to that far-flung vision of grace which sees a chosen company gathered and perfected in one age, that such may be the co-workers with Christ in His consummating work in the ages to come, on behalf of the rest. A thousand insuperable difficulties, involving God's character and impoverishing Calvary's power and scope, attach to man's pitiable attempt to "steady the ark of God." All such problems are solved and crowned with inextinguishable glory, when it is seen that the election of some is on the way to the inclusion of all. To the man first called alone this principle was enunciated, when God said to Abraham,

> "I will bless thee ... and thou shalt be a blessing ... and in thee shall all the families of the earth be blessed." (Genesis 12:1-3).

A.E. Saxby
London, England
God in Creation, Redemption, Judgment and Consummation
1922
(Reprinted by Bible Student's Press™, Windber, PA; 2010)

Appendix 12

FIFTEEN BOMBS
That Sank My Theological Ship

My first shock came when conducting evangelistic services in a community hall, I visited the home of a man, some of whose children had been saved at the meetings. I asked him if he would accept Christ as His personal Savior. He looked at the ground, and I hoped he would decide favorably, but when he looked up and spoke he set me thinking. His voice was slow and intense. "If the way you preach is right, then one of my boys is in hell now, and if that is where he is, I want to be with him …" That man wasn't fooling, he meant it!

My second shock came when a friend in Pennsylvania gave me a book called, *After the Thousand Years*,[1] by George F. Trench. Although I could not accept all the views of the author, I became convinced of two things, namely, that there is no word for "eternity" in the Greek or Hebrew Scriptures, and that the plainest teaching of the Word of God has been obscured by incorrect and inconsistent translation of the Greek word "aion." It cannot possibly mean "eternity," for consistency would force us into such senseless renderings as "the present eternity," and "before eternity" (see I Timothy 6:17; II Timothy 1:9; Titus 1:2). Furthermore, a consistent rendering of the word in Hebrews 9: 26 would give us the contradictory phrase: "at the conclusion of the eternity."

My third shock, the one that really jarred me loose from the binding tradition and the fear of men, came when a railroad engineer and a police sergeant, who had been impressed with my faithfulness in preaching the Word of God as I understood it, came to see me. We talked for nearly four hours. When they left I found I had used up all the heavy ammunition I had gathered in college, seminary and twenty years of conformity to the "Fundamentalist" and "Evangelical" hierarchy. I couldn't seem to be able to find their range, and when I did find it, my big gun jammed.

Fifteen bombs exploded on my deck, wrecking my fine theological system.

#1. If God will have all men to be saved, and if most men are lost, then how can God be supreme (I Timothy 2:3-4)?

#2. If Christ is the Propitiation for the sins of the whole world, did He die in vain for the lost (I John 2:2)?

#3. If God is going to reconcile the universe through Christ, how can some be tormented forever (Colossians 1:20)?

#4. How can God, in Christ, gather all things together as one while billions remain eternally estranged (Ephesians 1:10)?

#5. If all die in Adam, and a few are made alive in Christ, how can grace much more abound than sin (Romans 5:20)?

#6. If all men are condemned by one man's offense, why are not all men justified by one man's obedience (Roman 5:18)?

#7. If all die in Adam, why shall not all be made alive in Christ (I Corinthians 15:22)?

#8. How can every knee bow confessing Christ Lord, to God's glory, unless reconciled (Philippians 2:10-11)?

#9. If Christ only hath immortality, how can any of the dead be alive now (I Timothy 6:14-16; I Corinthians 15:53-54)?

#10. If the wicked go to hell as soon as they die, why are they raised and judged later (Revelation 20:11-15)?

#11. Since the lake of fire is the second death, what happens to the wicked when death is destroyed (I Corinthians 15:26)?

#12. If "forever" means "eternity" what does "forever and ever" mean?

#13. If God is love and has all power, will He not find a way to save all, or will His love ultimately fail (I Timothy 4:9-11)?

#14. If Christ is to reign "for ever and ever," what does it mean that He will deliver up the kingdom to the Father (Revelation 11:15; I Corinthians 15:24)?

#15. Will God ever actually become "All in all" (I Corinthians 15:28)?

It is amazing that so many doctrines not taught in Scripture have been branded as orthodox. As long as men accepted popery and priestcraft as orthodox, they were ignorant. But a fresh study of the Greek Scriptures at the time of the Reformation convinced believers that God was justifying sinners by faith, and consequently they broke with tradition and sought for a firm basis of truth in God's Word. You too will find new wonders in the Sacred Scriptures when you are ready to throw off the yoke of tradition and the fear of what people will say, and with a prayerful and teachable spirit, you study His Word and believe God!

V.E. Jacobson
Grace and Truth

Appendix 13

"THE DISPENSATION OF THE FULLNESS OF TIMES"

The inability of God's people to understand and accept the restitution of all things, which was spoken of by all the prophets since the world began, may be traced to three great faults in our traditional teaching.

Firstly, very, very few people are familiar with the truth that there is a coming age which the Bible names *"the dispensation of the fullness of times"* (Ephesians 1:10), and that that age above all others has been specially set aside for the work of reconciling all things in heaven and in earth and bringing all things into Christ.

The age, as I will point out presently, is the Age of the Ages. It is the greatest age of all ages and is the time in which the Almighty God brings to completion the unfailing Word spoken before time began, *"Let Us make man in Our image and after Our likeness."*

Secondly, God's people fail to see the final restitution of all things because they also fail to see the greatness of the work of Christ and the all-inclusive faith which God the Father has in that marvelous work of redemption.

Thirdly, and perhaps most important of all, is the failure of God's people to see that all things are of God, that He is working all things according to the Counsel of His own will. Nothing has *ever* gone wrong with the merciful purpose of God.

Once these three truths become clear to the spiritual mind of a devout child of God, then the mysteries of the ages disperse like mists before the rising sun and all the parts of the puzzle begin to fall into their appointed place to form a perfect blueprint of the progression of God's purpose through the ages …

Now I want you to pay particular attention to what God says regarding the mighty work of the age of the ages, the dispensation of the fullness of times. In it we are promised *"That in the dispensation of the fullness of times He might gather together in one all things in Christ, both which are in heaven, and which are on earth; even in Him"* (Ephesians 1:10).

I don't know how the Christian who disbelieves God's power to restore ail things is going to explain this mighty statement. Even blind unbelief can find no explanation for it, for there is no way around it. This is a clear statement of reconciliation definitely declaring that during the dispensation of the fullness of times all things are to be gathered into His Son, Jesus Christ. The statement is unconditional. There are no conditions attached in any way, shape or form. It is an edict of the Almighty, and it is saying with the greatest power and simplicity that He intends to restore absolutely everything and gather it all into the Prince Redeemer, Jesus Christ, whether it be things in heaven or things on earth.

G.R. Hawtin (1909-1994)
Creation, Redemption, and the Restitution of All Things
(Pages 71-72, 86-87)

Appendix 14

HIS SAVING WORK HAS ONLY JUST BEGUN

Because of what Jesus Christ has done, and will yet do in behalf of all mankind, the righteousness of God assures the salvation of all in due time. The "sacrificial work" of the Son of God has been finished on the cross (John 19:28-30). The "saving work" of the risen Son of God has only just begun and will continue until ALL have been delivered from sin and death …

Those who believe the gospel in this life, are saved for the eons or ages. They are justified by God's grace (Romans 3:24). They are reconciled to God (Colossians 1:21). They receive the Spirit of God, and are set free from the dominion of sin in their lives (Romans 8:9-11; 6:1-23). They will experience the deliverance of their bodies when Jesus Christ returns (I Corinthians 15:50-58). They will share the glory and the labor of their Savior during the coming eons (Ephesians 2:1-10; 3:8-11).

Those who do not believe in this life will be resurrected and judged at the time of the great white throne (Revelation 20:11-15). God will deal with them justly according to their deeds (Romans 2:1-16). Then those whose names are not in the book of life will suffer the second death (Revelation 20:15). This, however, is not their final end, for they will be MADE ALIVE at the conclusion of the eons when Jesus Christ abolishes the LAST ENEMY WHICH IS DEATH (I Corinthians 15:25-26). Then, they too will be justified (Romans 5:18-19), reconciled to God (Colossians 1:13-20), and be made immortal (I Corinthians 15:22; Romans 8:18-

23; II Timothy 1:9-11). Then ALL will be subjected to God the Father and God will be ALL IN ALL (I Corinthians 15:27-28).

Some believe and teach that Jesus Christ either cannot or will not save all. It is a source of sadness that so many who profess to know Him and to love Him should slander Him in this manner. Surely He does not lack the ability; He has already saved the chief of sinners (I Timothy 1:15). Neither does He lack the love; *"He died for all"* (II Corinthians 5:15). What He has promised in His Word He will certainly do. *"This is a faithful saying and worthy of all acceptation. For therefore we both labour and suffer reproach, because we trust in the living God, who is the Saviour of all men, specially of those that believe. These things command and teach"* (I Timothy 4:9-11).

Joseph E. Kirk (1904-1974)
The Good News Gospel

Appendix 15

THE JUST AND ULTIMATE PENALTY FOR SIN

Paul insists that Christ's death on the cross as a propitiation for sin, manifests the righteous judgment of God upon sin ...

Paul insists that God dealt fully and righteously with human sin in all its aspects. Accordingly, whatever debt, or price, or judgment, or penalty should have been met, He exacted in full from His own Beloved Son. In the crucified, God is dealing with the whole sin of the whole universe in holy love, in righteous judgment, and in redeeming grace. Recognizing this great fact, our Lord, hanging upon the cross, and ready to give up His spirit, spoke the word that, in His day, was regularly written across every receipted bill, *"Tetelestai," "Paid in full"* – (*"It is finished* [lit., "It is accomplished"]*"* – John 19:30). Christ on the cross demonstrates the love of God as nothing else ever did or can; yet He did more. The holy Son of mankind was making complete reparation to the holy and righteous throne of God.

But notice carefully what price He paid. If the just and ultimate penalty for sin is eternal torment, then Jesus can never be the Savior of anyone! He is not being eternally tormented. Again, if the just and ultimate penalty for sin is extermination, then Jesus can never be the Savior of anyone! He was not exterminated. Instead, He died for all; and, He is now in the glory as our advocate!

Loyal Hurley
The Outcome of Infinite Grace: Death Swallowed Up in Victory
(Pages 12-13)

Appendix 16

"I Am Going Mad!"

I would beg any of my brethren who still hesitate to preach a hope for mankind which they themselves cherish, to bear in mind what harm they may be doing by their silence ...

This book [*Salvator Mundi*] had an origin in an incident so pathetic that the story of it is well worth telling for its own sake; and is all the more worth telling because it may bring home to those who need it the warning which I have just uttered.

In. A.D. 1876, then, there had been in my congregation for many years, a poor and elderly workingman – not even a skilled artisan, but a man of proved character and fidelity, who filled some such slenderly paid office of trust as timekeeper, or gatekeeper, in a factory. He had never in his life, I should suppose, earned more than five and twenty shillings a week, and yet had contrived, by the aid of a good wife and industrious children, to live in comfort and in the respect of his neighbors. He was, as a man of his time and rank was sure to be, wholly uneducated, save that he had taught himself to read, and was fond of reading. But he had the precious habit of reflection, and would brood quietly and patiently over any great thought he met till it became his own, a veritable companion to his mind, an authoritative and molding influence on his life ...

There was no man in the whole circle of my acquaintance with whom I more enjoyed an hour's talk when it was to be had; for there was in his talk that spice of originality which is commonly to be found in that of men whose thoughts have been gathered not so much from books as from the working of their own minds. But he was very modest, very conscious of his own lack of culture, very fearful of intruding on the time of a busy man, or of seeming to presume on our relation as members of the same Church, and could not be induced to pay me more than a rare occasional visit.

Judge, then, of my surprise and concern, when, on a quiet evening in the summer of 1876, this calm, sensible, retiring man came, uninvited and unannounced, hastily into my room, and after wringing me by the hand, broke out with, "Mr. Cox, I'm going mad!" and sat, a picture of consternation, breathing hard and quick, as if it took the whole force of his will to hold himself in.

"But, Foster, what makes you think so?"

"May I tell you all about it, sir? It will be a great relief."

"Why, of course you may. I want to hear all about it, and to do anything I can for you."

"Well, sir, do you remember what a lovely evening we had on Sunday week? It was so fine that I did what I don't often do – went out for a walk instead of coming to Chapel. You see, sir, my hours of work all the week are so long, and I'm so tired when they're done, that I never get a chance of seeing the country unless I take a walk now and then on a fine Sunday. Well, I had had my walk through the fields, and my heart was full of praise 'for the beauty of the earth and the glory of the skies' (a quotation from one of our hymns), and was coming home over the river (Trent). When I got on the bridge the river was so lovely, with the bright sky reflected in it, that I folded my arms on the parapet, and looked up the stream a good while. And then I fell a-thinking. I thought within myself, 'How full the river is, and how fast it runs! What a deal of water runs through the bridge every day, and what a many years it's been running at pretty much the same pace.' And then I said to myself, 'Suppose every drop of water that ever ran through this bridge was to be brought back, and dammed up, beyond yon bend, into a vast lake, and then let down again a drop a minute. When all that water had run through the bridge once more, eternity would be no nearer an end than it is now.' And then I said, 'Suppose it was all brought back again, and let out a drop an hour, a drop a week, a drop a month, a drop a year – why, it would all run by, and God would be as young as He is today.' And then, sir, while I was trying to stretch my mind out, and get some notion of what the eternity of God was like, all of a sudden I bethought me of them poor souls down in the pit! And my head reeled, and my heart stood still, and I cried out quite loud, 'O, my God, can it be true that after all those dreadful years their torment would be no nearer an end than it is now?' The thought was too horrible, it was too much for me, sir; but I couldn't shake it out of my head, and I can't. It has haunted me ever since, and it's well-nigh killing me. I can't hear a bell toll, or a clock tick, but what I go off calculating, and calculating and calculating, just as I did on the bridge – so many ticks, so many years, and the end no nearer than before. I can't eat; I can't sleep; I can get no good or comfort of my life. In fact, sir, I'm going mad; and if you can't help me, I shall be mad before long."

As my poor friend concluded his sad tale with this wistful but almost hopeless appeal, he lifted his thick brows, and let me see the dull lire of misery and fear burning in his eyes. I confess I was as astonished that he should have listened to me for years without apprehending that, for me at least, no such dreadful dogma was taught by Christ and his Apostles as I was grieved by his misery and despair. For though I had never attempted a formal demonstration of "the larger hope" in a series of discourses, I had always assumed it, and had let it shape and color all my teaching, while I had often inferred it and given explicit expression to it when the text in hand led that way. I spent an hour with him in going through the leading passages of the New Testament which bore on the question, and in answering any difficulties or objections which he brought forward. And at the end of that memorable hour he went away a new man, so transformed in appearance as well as in spirit, that anyone who had seen him enter and leave my house would have had much ado to have known him for the same man.

When he had gone I could not but reflect that if he had failed to gather the truth I believed, the hope I cherished, from the sermons he had chanced to hear me preach, there might be other members of my congregation to whom it would be as new and helpful as to him, and hence I resolved that this should be my theme at the next session of my Bible Class. In due course the lectures were delivered, discussed and published in *Salvator Mundi*.

Samuel Cox (1826-1893)
Salvator Mundi: Or, Is Christ the Saviour of All Men?
(1877)

Appendix 17

THE SALVATION OF THE UNBELIEVER

The case of Thomas is an example of the overpowering force of evidence where faith is wanting [lacking]. No man can long withstand the testimony of his senses, even when his interests are opposed. But today the doubting Thomases are offered no proof to correct their credulous questions. It is either sheer unfounded faith or fatal unbelief.

The tangible proofs given to support the proclamation of the kingdom affords a rich field for the study of the effect of evidence on the human heart. The unbeliever will be saved by sight. He will yield to the force of facts. He will be convinced by logic. What evidence is most suited for this purpose? In our Lord's ministry we can see both the helps and the hindrances offered by the senses. The consideration of a few cases will reveal what most moves men and what makes them obstinate.

The rich young man was hindered by his possessions. The Samaritans were helped by the Lord's words. The resurrection of Lazarus led many Jews to rely on His acts. These illustrate God's method in the judgment of the unbeliever. He removes hindrances – no earthly acquisitions interfere with the decisions of the heart, for both heaven and earth flee from the face of Him Who sits on the throne. He works the greatest possible miracle, by raising them from the dead. He reads the inmost secret of their hearts. He appears in their very presence in soul-dismaying splendor. They cannot doubt His power or His perfections, and no motive remains to lead them to deceive themselves.

The judgment of unbelievers takes place in the interval between the passing of this present earth and the creation of the new. Every tie which bound them to the earth has been burned up. They are the subjects of the most astounding miracle ever wrought, having been raised from the dead. They are in the presence of the Divine Majesty. Their secrets are bared to His awful gaze. The character of their judgment, being adjusted to their acts, not simply as to severity but so as to correct them, will reveal God's purpose to save and reconcile them to Himself.

A.E. Knoch (1874-1965)
All in All: The Goal of the Universe
(Page 90, 91)

Appendix 18

FULLY VICTORIOUS LOVE

If this love is not finally victorious over all evil, then God finally is not a God of grace, all-loving and all-powerful. If the purpose and plan of God are not finally fulfilled, then obviously God has failed. Finally, God's will has not been done. And in this case, what kind of God is this? Certainly not the God of grace claimed by the entire New Testament. And when God is so disgraceful, we're left with an alternative: either the threat of a meaningless hell, in which people can choose to be tortured for all eternity to no good purpose; or else, rejecting a meaningless hell, a meaningless life without any God – a life that may follow "the paths of glory" for a very little while but then finally ends only in the grave. If death and the grave have the last word, then life – by definition – is meaningless. It isn't going anywhere. And a meaningless life makes people mean. Ultimately having no future, we may as well get all we can while we can. Thus meaninglessness doth make vicious little vermin of us all. Rats, in other words.

In our sillier moments we may try to tell ourselves that the gift of life should be satisfying enough for anyone who has known it, and that it's selfish of us to want more. Save this beautiful thought. Save it for the four-year-old with leukemia you may run into. And in the meantime, take note of this from Paul:

"Now if Christ be preached that He rose from the dead, how say some among you that there is no resurrection of the dead? But if there be no resurrection of the dead, then is Christ not risen: And if Christ be not risen,

then is our preaching vain, and your faith is also vain … If in this life only we have hope in Christ, we are of all men most miserable" (I Corinthians 15:12-14, 19).

But of course in this case everyone is to be pitied. For the more beautiful life may have been, the sadder it'll be to leave it. And this sadness is easy to feel long before the end. It really isn't very good news to tell someone, "It just doesn't get any better than this."

But Christians are a people who believe firmly in God's grace, and therefore they are persuaded that God's purpose and plan will finally be fulfilled. And that plan and purpose is good news – the best possible news – for all. Once more, the words of Paul:

"In Whom we have redemption through His blood, the forgiveness of sins, according to the riches of His grace; Wherein He hath abounded toward us in all wisdom and prudence; Having made known unto us the mystery of His will, according to His good pleasure which He hath purposed in Himself: That in the dispensation of the fulness of times He might gather together in one all things in Christ, both which are in heaven, and which are on earth; even in Him" (Ephesians 1:7-10).

This is faith's final answer to evil, then, the answer that the universe, everything and everyone in heaven and earth, will finally be brought into a unity in Christ … This answer does assure us that finally all evil – all sin, death, and suffering – will be overcome. And therefore faith can also say with Paul,

"For I reckon that the sufferings of this present time are not worthy to be compared with the glory which shall be revealed in us" (Romans 8:18).

The late William Barclay, the great Scottish Bible teacher and scholar, tells us in his autobiography, "I believe that in the end all men will be gathered into the love of God." And he goes on to point out that in supporting this case, "The New Testament itself is not in the least afraid of the word all." Especially in Paul's writings there are plenty of places where he can't seem to cram enough "all's" into what he wants to say. For example, he looks forward to the time when,

*"For He must reign, till He hath put **all** enemies under His feet. The last enemy that shall be destroyed is death … And when **all** things shall be*

*subdued unto Him, then shall the Son also Himself be subject unto Him that put **all** things under Him, that God may be **All** in **all**"* (I Corinthians 15:25-26, 28).

So all in all, the Bible tells us we know through faith in Christ that God will finally be All in all. The Bible's last word is *"all."* Sin, evil, suffering, death, and a literal hell are finally conquered by this literal *"all"*

*"The grace of our Lord Jesus Christ be with you **all**. Amen."* (Revelation 22:21).

That's the Bible's punch line …

And surely we can expect at least as much from God as God expects from us. Again, the words of Jesus:

"But I say unto you, Love your enemies, bless them that curse you, do good to them that hate you, and pray for them which despitefully use you, and persecute you; that ye may be the children of your Father which is in heaven: for He maketh His sun to rise on the evil and on the good, and sendeth rain on the just and on the unjust. Be ye therefore perfect, even as your Father which is in heaven is perfect" (Matthew 5:44-45, 48).

Robert L. Short
Short Mediations on the Bible and Peanuts
(1991)

Appendix 19

ALL MEN WILL BE MADE RIGHTEOUS THROUGH JESUS CHRIST

Two persons, two acts, and two results affecting the entire human race are brought before us in this passage of Scripture (Romans 5:18-19). Adam's disobedience and its race-wide, life-destroying result, presents a dark and distressing situation. The obedience of Jesus Christ and the race-wide, life-giving result is bright and glorious.

Is it not strange that the distressing part of this passage is usually believed without hesitation, but the bright and glorious part is disbelieved? Conditions and limitations are forced into the part dealing with the life and righteousness that comes to all through Jesus Christ, until its plain statements are flatly contradicted. Lack of faith in what the Scriptures clearly state, rather than lack of intelligence to grasp the meaning, has always been one of the greatest hindrances to the correct understanding of God's word …

Adam's one offense brought the condemnation of death upon all mankind (Romans 5:12). None escape this condemnation (*"For as in Adam all die"* – I Corinthians 15:22). THUS ALSO, the obedience of Jesus Christ will bring justifying of life unto all mankind (*"even so in Christ shall all be made alive"* – I Corinthians 15:22).

The matter of faith or acceptance is not introduced on either side in this passage. The subject is not eonian ["eternal"] life; neither is it the salvation of the elect. When these are being discussed, faith, and acceptance have their place …

The point being emphasized is the fact that all mankind shall be constituted righteous through the obedience of Jesus Christ, just as surely as they were constituted sinners through the disobedience of Adam. This fact is stated in verse 18, and the inspired explanation follows in verse 19. Notice how the *"for"* links the two verses together …

Jesus Christ came into the world to SAVE the world. He will not fail in the slightest degree. His death, and resurrection life will prove effective for all in due time. Man's present failure to comprehend and believe in the success of the Sacrificial and Saving work of Jesus Christ will not take away in the least from His triumph and success. God wills that *"all men be saved"* (I Timothy 2:3-6; 4:9-11). Our risen, living Lord and Savior is equal to the task. He will not fail.

Does this deny what the Scriptures actually teach concerning the future judgment and condemnation of the wicked? Absolutely not! There will be judgment … (Romans 2:1-16; Revelation 20:11-15). But thanks be to God, beyond that there will be justification of life and righteousness for all mankind through Jesus Christ our Lord (See I Corinthians 15:20-28).

Joseph E. Kirk (1904-1974)
Will All Mankind Be Constituted Righteous Through Jesus Christ?

Appendix 20

THE QUESTION OF HITLER

Some of My Own Attitudes Towards the Example of Hitler that So Many Cite So Often

How many of you believe that you are a more worthy candidate for salvation than Hitler was? Bear in mind that, unlike Hitler, none of us here have the power of a modern state at our disposal, so the amount of harm we can do is in that sense limited by the grace of God. If we get angry with someone in this forum, for example, we might say something nasty, but we are in no position to send the Gestapo after the person who offends us. Nor are we in a position, such as Hitler was, where our own weaknesses and prejudices can easily be transformed into political terror. The same weaknesses and prejudices may in fact be there, but we do not have available to us the same means of expressing them that Hitler had available to him.

"Power corrupts, and absolute power corrupts absolutely," said Lord Acton. But few of us have experienced even the temptations of political power, much less the temptations of "absolute" tyrannical power. So how many are utterly confident that in Hitler's precise circumstances you would have come off any better than he did?

First, I strongly suspect that Hitler was in a far more hopeful condition at the end of his earthly life, after all of his evil plans and ambitions had come to ruin, than he was at any time previously … Historians believe that Hitler committed suicide at the end, though no one really knows this for sure. But even if he did commit suicide, the very despair or sense of defeat that sometimes leads to suicide can just as easily lead to repentance and to a voluntary submission of one's will to God. If I were to speculate, therefore, I would guess that Hitler, like the terrorist Saul of Tarsus, may have been far closer to the kingdom of God, even during his earthly life, than many professing Christians who continue to harbor hatreds, secret resentments, and petty jealousies in their own hearts. For though Hitler's hatred of the Jews was no less intense than Saul's hatred of Christians, it was at least out in the open where it could be dealt with effectively.

Second, I have no confidence at all that in Hitler's shoes I would have fared any better than he did ... I have a hard time imagining myself masterminding genocide ... I have a hard time seeing myself as an evil monster. But here I would make two observations.

(1) I was reared in one of the most loving families that you could possibly imagine. My mother constantly cultivated a sense of empathy in her children, constantly taught us to consider the other person's feelings, constantly asked questions like, "How would you feel if ..." Had I been switched as a baby and placed in a very different home, perhaps that of a white racist family, or had I been exposed to various kinds of physical and sexual abuse as a child, or had I been exposed to the same forces that shaped Hitler's personality, I have no confidence that I would have turned out any better than he did.

(2) Even as an adult with all the advantages I have had, I have done some pretty rotten and some pretty selfish things. So if I were suddenly thrust into truly terrifying circumstances – like armed combat, for example – or if I were required to live with a persistent fear for the safety of my family, or if I were to come to believe, however irrationally, that a group of people were a threat to our nation and to our very way of life, I see no reason why I might not gradually be seduced – these things usually come about gradually – into some truly monstrous acts ... I am capable of all sin, and only the grace of God has kept me from horrendous ones.

Third, I have every confidence that the difference between Hitler and me is not a simple matter of my having made better free choices than he did. I believe in free will, but I also accept the Pauline assertion that our destiny *"is not of him that willeth, nor of him that runneth, but of God that sheweth mercy"* (Romans 9:16). We are guilty of self-righteousness if we start to think so-and-so (Hitler in this example) is worse off than we are in God's eyes. Self-righteousness or spiritual pride is one of the most pernicious of all sins – which is why, I believe, that Jesus came down upon it so harshly. Put it together with a heavy dose of fear – such as fear of everlasting punishment – and you have a prescription for truly monstrous acts. Unfortunately, some of the greatest theologians in the Western tradition, men still widely revered as heroes of the faith, have in fact supported acts of terror that are every bit as evil as Hitler's own actions were.

Why suppose that the weakness and fear that led Augustine to support the persecution of the Donatists, or the weakness and fear that led the religious leaders in Geneva to burn Servetus at the stake (over green wood so that it took three hours for him to be pronounced dead), or the weakness and fear that led the Calvinists in Zurick to drown Anabaptists in a sort of hideous parody of their belief in believer's baptism – why suppose that any of this was essentially different from the weakness and fear that led Hitler into some of his own most monstrous acts? The only difference I can discern is that you can't do as much damage with a sword and a Medieval torture chamber as you can with guns, airplanes and gas chambers.

I offer this not as an argument for anything, but merely as a description of some of my own attitudes and beliefs.

Thomas Talbott
(Author of *The Inescapable Love of God*)
Willamette University (website, 2000)

Appendix 21

ETERNAL TORMENT

Q: If the smoke of their torment *"ascendeth up for ever and ever"* and *"they have no rest day nor night,"* doesn't this indicate eternal suffering?

A: Revelation 14:10-11; 20:10; 22:5 contain words that have been corrupted and changed by traditional religious dogma. Those words are the Greek *"basanizo/basanismos"* and *"aion."* By simply opening any Greek-English lexicon, you will see sizeable differences between the definitions of the Greek words I mentioned, and the definitions of the English words that were used to translate those Greek words. However, to be thorough, I will discuss not only the differences between the Greek and English definitions, but I will also use Scripture to define these words.

Basanizo/Basanismos

In Revelation 14:10, the word *"basanizo"* is translated as *"tormented"* (past tense verb).

In Revelation 14:11, the word *"basanismos"* is translated as *"torment"* (noun).

In Revelation 20:10, the word *"basanizo"* is translated as *"tormented"* (past tense verb).

Both of these words come from the root *"basanos,"* which is defined by Strong as "a touchstone." Webster defines the word "touchstone" as:

1. A stone by which metals are examined; a black, smooth, glossy stone ...

2. Any test or criterion by which the qualities of a thing are tried; as money, the touchstone of common honesty."

This might strike you as interesting considering that the definition of the Greek word that was translated as "torment," not only has nothing to do with eternal conscious torment, but it is actually a process that tests purity. So we can see that to be tormented in these verses is compared to being rubbed upon a touchstone.

A good contextual scriptural definition of the word *"basanizo"* can be found in II Peter 2:8:

"(For that righteous man dwelling among them, in seeing and hearing, vexed [basanizo] his righteous soul from day to day with their unlawful deeds;)"

This passage talks about Lot dwelling in Sodom. In this verse, we see that Lot, even though he is called *"righteous,"* receives the same *"torment"* that those in the *"lake of fire"* receive. Of course, as we can see, Lot's righteous soul is only being tested, and is not receiving eternal conscious torment.

You might be saying, "Ok, so even if they are being tested and not barbequed, this is still happening *'for ever and ever'"* That's where the other word *"aion"* comes in.

Aion

The concept of "eternity" is something that can be expected to be confused by the human mind. There are many theories about what "eternity" is. Some theories say eternity is "never ending time" while some say the complete opposite; "timelessness."

Regardless of what the theories say, when you find a concept that is so commonly misunderstood by the human mind in a book that was translated by humans, a giant red flag should go up in your head. You should immediately sit down and study this topic, knowing that the translators weren't superhuman, but that they were humans just like so many others that confuse the topic of eternity.

The word *"ever"* in Revelation 14:11; 20:10; 22:5 was translated from the word *"aion."* *"Aion"* is defined by Strong as "an age."

Does an age last forever? Let's check the Scriptures:

> *"Who hath saved us, and called us with an holy calling, not according to our works, but according to His own purpose and grace, which was given us in Christ Jesus before the world* [aion] *began"* (II Timothy 1:9).

> *"Now all these things happened unto them for ensamples: and they are written for our admonition, upon whom the ends of the world* [aion] *are come"* (I Corinthians 10:11).

So we see that an age (*aion*) begins and ends. In fact, *"smoke rising up for ever and ever"* begins and ends in just one short chapter in Revelation.

In Revelation 18:10-17, the Great Whore of Babylon is destroyed in just one hour:

> *"For in one hour so great riches is come to nought ..."* (:17).

> *"And cried when they saw the smoke of her burning ..."* (:18).

Now, the smoke of Babylon's burning was visible in :18, however, by Revelation 19:3, we see that the smoke rose in the past tense:

> *"And again they said, Alleluia. And her smoke rose up for ever and ever."*

So, we see that unless there was an endless amount of time between Revelation 18:18 and Revelation 19:3, *"for ever and ever"* does not mean eternity.

Aaron Locker
Hollidaysburg, PA

Appendix 22

THE FIRE OF GOD
and the Second Death

THE PURPOSE OF DIVINE FIRE

The basic purpose of the divine fire of God is to cleanse, purify, purge, temper and change. It is to rid of impurities, of filth, of undesirable elements. There is no better way to deal with filth than to deal with it by fire. The divine fire will burn up all the governments, institutions, systems and fruitage of the carnal mind. It will melt all the customs, cultures, traditions and practices of society and make of this earth a new earth wherein dwells righteousness. Every man's work will eventually be tested in this fire. The fire will try every man's work of what sort it is. If you and I build into our walls wood, hay and stubble, that fire will find it out, and the walls will come tumbling down.

When God turns on the heat, the blazing light of His Spirit and Word – some things begin to change! The fire is never sent to destroy the *person*, but to purge out all that hinders and separates him from his God, to consume the pride, arrogance, hostility, defiance and rebellion of the flesh, the carnal mind.

More than three centuries ago when the Black Plague swept through London, England, more than 68,000 men, women and children were sickened with the putrid fever, suffered nameless agonies, passed into delirium, sometimes with convulsions, and then died. Before the end of the terrible nightmare of anguish and death, what was thought to be an even greater tragedy occurred. The city caught fire, the whole heavens were ablaze as the Great Fire destroyed more than 13,200 homes and 89 churches. Most of the city, which was built largely of wood, lay in ashes. Wonder of wonders! As soon as the last dying embers cooled and the smoke cleared, the inhabitants of the city discovered that the Plague had been stayed! Not another person died of the epidemic. The Plague never returned. The fire had killed the bacteria-carrying fleas and rats that caused the Plague. It took a fire to do it!

Make no mistake! *"Our God is a consuming fire"* (Hebrews 12:29).

THE SECOND DEATH

The book of Revelation is a book of symbols. In the introduction to this marvelous book the beloved John explains,

> *"The revelation of Jesus Christ, which God gave unto Him, to show unto His servants things which must shortly come to pass; and He sent and signified it by His angel unto His servant John"* (Revelation 1:1).

The word "signified" is from the Greek *"semaino"* meaning to indicate or communicate by means of signs and symbols. The meanings of all the symbols of the Revelation are given, either in the book itself, or elsewhere in the Scriptures. He tells us exactly what certain things are. In Revelation 20:14 God tells us exactly what the Second Death is.

> *"And death and hell were cast into the Lake of Fire. THIS IS THE SECOND DEATH."*

Now let me make this a little plainer. Definitions of men can be given backward. For instance, the definition, "An island is a tract of land completely surrounded by water," can be given thus: "A tract of land completely surrounded by water is an island." This is but another way of stating the same fact. It does not, in any way, change the meaning.

Now let us try this on the definition of the Second Death. The Bible states it thus:

> *"Death and hell were cast into the Lake of Fire. THIS IS the Second Death."*

Now let us turn this around for clarity.

"The Second Death IS death and hell cast into the Lake of Fire."

Therefore we have exactly the same meaning either way it is stated. What is the Second Death? It is the first death and hell cast into the Lake of Fire! This fact is very important. The Second Death is not merely the Lake of Fire. The Second Death is not men being tortured for ever in the Lake of Fire. God has made it very simple and plain. The Second Death is the first death and hell *"cast into the Lake of Fire."* That is God's definition.

Can we now open the eyes of our understanding to see that everything cast into the Lake of Fire pertains to *death*? Death itself is cast into the Lake of Fire. Hell, the realm of the dead, is cast into the Lake of Fire. And those whose names are not written in the Book of Life, those who are dead, in trespasses and in sins, who inhabit hell, are cast into the Lake of Fire. That is the end of death and hell and sin, for God shall destroy death in the Lake of Fire, He shall burn up hell in the Lake of Fire, and He shall consume sin and rebellion in the Lake of Fire.

THE DEATH OF DEATHS

How I long to see the end of sin and death and hell! The time is coming, praise His name, when God shall be *"All in all,"* and there shall be neither sin, nor sinners, nor death, nor hell. It is clear that God does not destroy men in the Lake of Fire, nowhere does it say that, for that would be a contradiction of terms. How can you destroy death by creating death? How can you abolish death by bringing men under the power of eternal death from which there is no escape? Oh, no, it is not men who are destroyed in the Lake of Fire – it is sin and death and hell that are destroyed.

"And the last enemy that shall be destroyed is death" (I Corinthians 15:26).

Thus, *"the Lake of Fire"* is nothing more nor less than the death of deaths!

The following words by Ray Prinzing give fresh insight into this wonderful truth:

The question arises, "Is the Second Death the same kind of death as the first?" Many people think that it is a repetition of the first, and that the results are the same, while its action is more severe and cruel, and destructive, being by fire. And some Christians add very sorrowfully, "and from this Second Death there is no resurrection, it is an endless torment in agony," BUT NOT SO! For God's seconds are never duplicates of the first: they are always better, higher, and more powerful than the firsts, and used to counter-balance all the action of the firsts, and MUCH MORE – He always saves the best until last.

All Bible statements prove that the two deaths are absolutely *unalike*, and that the two are opposite and antagonistic. The Second Death undoes all the work of the first death in the same manner that the last Adam undid all the work of the first Adam. Not to nullify the purpose being wrought out by the plan of God in the firsts, but to bring a release from the firsts in a MUCH MORE manner of majesty and glory and power and scope of coverage, into the greater and glorious things of God.

Creation was made subject to vanity for a purpose! Sin was allowed for wise ends, but when those ends have been secured it will have to cease to exist. The purpose is not nullified, but the means whereby the purpose has been executed shall be done away. Discipline is a means to an end, but not an end in itself, for,

> "*afterward it yieldeth the peaceable fruit of righteousness*" (Hebrews 12:11).

The first Adam died to God and righteousness, and became alive unto sin. The last Adam died unto sin (Romans 6:10), and lives unto God, and so fulfills all righteousness. The first made all men sinners, the last makes all men righteous. The lives and the deaths of the two Adams are thus greatly contrasting the one to the other. The First Death was a transition from life to death, the Second Death is a transition from corruption to incorruption, from mortality to immortality – transformed from the carnal mind to the spiritual mind, which is life and peace, which transformation is wrought by a dying out to the one realm, to come alive to the higher realm. The Second Death is prepared to purge out and burn away sin and its results, and so doing cleanse God's entire universe.

Death came as an enemy, the fruitage of an act of disobedience that turned man away from God and into the realm of carnality, minding self and flesh. Now God makes death overcome itself. It is by death that death is rendered powerless, and there arises an up-springing, a new life. It takes death to destroy death, and thus Christ did, *"taste death for every man … that through death He might destroy him that had the power of death, that is, the devil; and deliver them who through fear of death were all their lifetime subject to bondage"* (Hebrews 2:9, 14-15).

No More Death

At last shall be fulfilled the beautiful promise:

"And I heard a great voice out of heaven saying, Behold, the tabernacle of God is with men, and He will dwell with them, and they shall be His people, and God Himself shall be with them, and be their God. And God shall wipe away all tears from their eyes; and there shall be no more death, neither sorrow, nor crying, neither shall there be any more pain: for the former things are passed away. And He that sat upon the throne said, Behold, I make all things new. And He said unto me, Write: for these words are true and faithful" (Revelation 21:3-5).

Whatever we hold as the nature of the death state, may we let this truth sink deep into our hearts: death is to be abolished. The ringing declaration, *"The last enemy that shall be destroyed is death"* (I Corinthians 15:26), overthrows the whole structure of accepted, but unproved theology which shuts up the mass of the human race in "eternal death." When the "last" enemy is abolished it is self-evident that none remains. Those wretched religionists who demand the endlessness of death, who argue for eternal torment in the Lake of Fire, the Second Death, do err, not knowing the Scriptures nor the power of God. The Lake of Fire MUST end because death and hell are cast into it, which is the Second Death, and in the end,

"there shall be N-O M-O-R-E D-E-A-T-H."

No more death! No more first death. No more Second Death. No more of any kind of death. To say there is no more death is to say that there are no more sinners, for sinners are DEAD MEN, dead in trespasses and in sins. To say there is no more death is to say that God has not "burned up" all the wicked and left them dead, or in hell, for as long as any creature of God is in a state of death, death is not abolished. To say there is no more death is to say there is no more hell, for hell is "the realm of the dead." To say there is no more death is to say there is no more a Lake of Fire, for the Lake of Fire *IS* the Second Death. To say there is no more death is to say there is no more sin, for *"the wages of sin is DEATH."*

What a universe of truth is contained in three little words: NO MORE DEATH! This grand truth seems to be almost unknown in the Church systems. Although the very climax and fulfillment of all revelation, it has been eclipsed by human perversions. As a result the "God" of the popular Churches has lost the essential attributes of Deity. He is like the foolish man who started to build but could not finish. Man's theology brings nothing to a conclusion. It attains no definite goal. Sin, suffering, and disobedience are never conquered. Death is never destroyed. Redemption is never fully secured. God is compelled to work an eternal miracle in order to maintain a never-ending eyesore in His creation, once so subject, so sinless, and so good. He has to eternally keep His great foot on the lid of hell; for if even one of the devils should get out there would be hell everywhere!

But death in all its forms shall be destroyed until it shall be said, *"There is no more death!"* Jesus is Conqueror! Then shall *every* creature in the universe bow and in glad chorus sing,

> *"O death, where is thy sting? O grave, where is thy victory? The sting of death is sin; and the strength of sin is the law. But thanks be to God, which giveth us the victory through our Lord Jesus Christ"* (I Corinthians 15:55-57).

J. Preston Eby
(A small abridgement taken from *The Savior of the World* series)

Appendix 23

GOD AND FATHER OF ALL

"One God and Father of all, who is above all, and through all, and in you all" (Ephesians 4:6).

If there is any point of doctrine that was absolutely new in the preaching of Jesus Christ, it is the truth which He was the first to bring out into the light, that God is our Father. How prominent a topic this is in His gospel.

First, it means a great deal more than that God is merely our friend. He is related to us as a parent to a child. There is something more than mere good will; there is a kindred tie that binds the two together. God feels for us a paternal affection that is as much stronger than any which we find in the family relation upon earth, and as much purer, too, as God is greater and more holy than man.

He sympathizes with us as the father of the prodigal, in the parable of old, sympathized with his erring son. In the New Testament, God is represented as calling upon us, although sinners still. He is represented as calling upon us to recognize Him in that peculiar and endearing relation, and to be assured of His paternal love – in all prayers to address Him as our Father in heaven and in all our service of Him to be His followers *"as dear children."*

I believe you will bear me witness, when I say that this is the distinguishing idea of the gospel, the one which Jesus Christ and His apostles always place first and foremost – I mean when speaking of the relation between our Creator and ourselves.

Second, you will also see that it is only carrying out this idea to its full extent to say, as Paul does in the words of our text, that God is the Father of all. He holds the same relation, in this respect, to the whole human race. His divine paternity is not of a partial nature, is not confined to a certain class of men, but universal, as all His other essential relations are.

Everybody would feel at once the absurdity of supposing that God was the "Sovereign" only of a certain class of men, or the "Judge" only of a few, or the "Creator" only of a part; and it would be equally absurd to restrict His paternal relation in this way. *"One God and Father of all, who is above all, and through all, and in you all."* If He is the Father of mankind, as the gospel asserts, the very nature of the case shows that He must be the Father of all. This is the doctrine of our text.

Third, we may contemplate this truth in its direct bearing upon the relation which God holds to all mankind, as their father – *"one God and Father of all.*

It is a very significant fact, recorded in the first chapter of Genesis, that when man was brought into being, *"God created him in His Own image,"* that is, as His child, imparted to him His Own nature, as a parent does to his offspring; fixed that relationship in his very being at creation. Let us observe what this important truth amounts to.

Every person that lives, or that ever did live, in this world, *every* individual whom God has created, has a Father in heaven. He may be a sinner; he may be as guilty as the prodigal in the parable; he may be alienated from his Father, dead in trespasses and sins, but there still is this indestructible relation "of Father and child" existing between him and his Creator. This is what Paul means. On another occasion, he told the idolatrous Athenians that they, even they, were *"the offspring of God,"* although they were utterly estranged from Him.

Fourth, we do not forget that there is one sense in which God is not the Father of all. There are many who have not been regenerated, and who are not, in this spiritual sense, His children; that is, they do not resemble God in their character.

Christ said to the Jews, for instance, *"If God were your Father, ye would love me."* *"Ye are of your father the devil, and the works of your father ye will do."* And so in several other passages of Scripture, God is spoken of as the Father only of those who believe; but in all these cases the meaning is too obvious to need illustration. We know they relate only to spiritual character, not to the persons themselves.

What we wish to say is that, underneath this spiritual relationship, there must be a natural relationship that binds all mankind to God. If God created them all in His own image, He is of course their Father in the natural sense. *"One God and Father of all, who is above all, and through all, and in you all."*

Finally, we have already observed that there is another bearing in which the same general truth may be considered. As all mankind have one and the same Father in heaven, they have a common relationship with one another, as well as with Him. They are all brethren; they form but one family in the constitution fixed by their Creator.

It is a most important truth, that all the different classes of people, from the lowest to the highest, from the best to the worst, of all nations, colors, characters, and conditions, are bound together by an eternal blood-relationship, which they cannot sever, though they may sin against it. This is the doctrine of Paul, when he says, *"God hath made of one blood all nations of men, to dwell on all the face of the earth."* Whether civilized or savage, black, or white, or red, freemen or bondmen, saints or sinners, all were created brethren, just as much as the children in your family were born in that affinity; and, in the sight of God and duty, they never can become other than brethren, let them disregard the fraternal obligation as much as they may.

Hosea Ballou (1771-1852)

Is God Schizophrenic?

Ask any Christian why they believe God will torment people forever, and you'll usually get the response, "God loves all men, but He is also just." While it is certainly true that God is both love and justice, modern theology perverts both of these wonderful attributes of God by creating a dualistic natured god – a god incapable of loving and executing His justice at the same time.

The Bible declares in I John 4:8 that *"God is love."* When the Apostle John was thinking of a perfect phrase to describe God's love, notice he didn't say, "God is loving." All of us know that God does loving acts, but to John, this description was insufficient to describe the depths and perfection of the love of God. Humans are capable of showing love, but God is much more than man. John was saying that God is more than just loving deeds. He *"is"* love. In other words, the very essence (or character) of God *"is love."* He is always love – 24/7. In every circumstance and in every place, *"God is love."* There is no time, ever, when God is not love. Do you believe this? The Bible gives us a beautiful description of God's love in I Corinthians 13.

"Love is patient and kind. Love knows neither envy nor jealousy. Love is not forward and self-assertive, nor boastful and conceited. Love does not

behave unbecomingly, nor seek to aggrandize (boast of greatness) itself, nor blaze out in passionate anger, nor brood over wrongs. It finds no pleasure in injustice done to others, but joyfully sides with the truth. It knows how to be silent. It is full of trust, full of hope, full of patient endurance."

When reading the above passage, try this: every time the word "love" is used, take it out and replace it with the word "God." Since God "is" love, God is also patient and kind. He also is not envious or jealous. He is not forward and self-assertive, nor boastful and conceited. He does not behave unbecomingly, nor seeks to make His name great at the expense of others. He does not blaze out in passionate, uncontrolled anger, nor broods over wrongs.

Let us now look at the doctrine of eternal torment in the light of the great truth concerning God's great love. If it is true that God is always love (and He is!), how do we then explain the doctrine of eternal torment? One hard-line reformer, Jonathan Edwards wrote, "Hell is God's perfect hatred without love." Edwards knew that the doctrine of never-ending punishments was incompatible with God's love, which is why he had to remove any suggestion that God's love could reach into the lowest "hell." But how can this be? If God can do nothing apart from His love, how do we explain the fact that God supposedly torments most of His creation for all eternity for no apparent purpose? If God's punishments never end, then what purpose do they hold for the offender – what betterment to the sinner? If there is no intent on correcting the behavior of the offender, then the only purpose this punishment could serve would be to either satisfy God's own sense of justice or to teach the poor sinner an "eternal" lesson. [I]n either case, this would be a selfish act because God would be thinking solely of Himself.

God could not have the best interest of the sinner at heart if His punishments continued without end. Isn't love being concerned for the welfare of another? I Corinthians 13:5 says, *"Love (God) seeks not its (His) own things."* The very essence of love is the idea that it is purely unselfish – it seeks not its own. If God acts in a manner prescribed by the majority of the Church by torturing most of His creation forever – with no thought whatsoever of rehabilitation for the sinner – how then can this be love? As an earthly father, no matter how bad and rebellious my children act, I could never punish them simply out of anger and vengeance – for to do so would be selfish and unloving. And if I did, could it be said that I truly loved my children? If I inflict severe pain on my children simply to teach them a lesson, with absolutely no intent on correcting their behavior, what kind of father would I be? And what kind of Father would God be if He acted in this same manner? God would not be a loving God if He acted thus toward most of His created beings. Does an earthly parent have more capacity to love than God? What loving parent on the face of the earth would ever do (to their own children) the kinds of horrors that Christians ascribe to God? Isn't God's love far greater than the love that earthly parents have for their own children? The idea of "eternal" hell shows that we believe in a god who acts simply to satisfy his own need for justice and revenge. And if this is the case, then God is NOT love, at least to the great majority of those He torments "eternally."

If the Bible is true when it says that God is love – then God must love at all times – not just in this short lifespan He gives us. Didn't Jesus Himself tell us to love our enemies (Matthew 5:44)? Didn't Paul teach us that if our enemies hunger and thirst, we should give them food and drink (Romans 12:20)? Does this only apply to a man's short lifespan on the earth? Does God's love stop after a man dies?

An acquaintance of mine tried to defend the doctrine of "eternal" torment by saying that "God only loves in memory – not physically." I'm not even sure what that is supposed to mean. Where is that in the Bible? Doesn't the apostle John tell us to "… *love not in word only, but in deed and truth*" (I John 3:18)? How can God only love in memory, and not in deeds?

Some justify the lie of "eternal" torment by saying that "God's ways are higher than ours." In other words, "God can do whatever He pleases and it is not our business to question God." God can certainly do whatsoever He pleases to whomever He pleases. However, in anything God does, He cannot contradict His own Word. If God commands us to love and forgive *"seventy times seven"* and show love to our most hated enemy, then God must do the same. God will never expect us to do something that He Himself isn't willing to do. If God tells us to keep on forgiving, then God will also keep forgiving – even after this life is over.

In order to get around the irrefutable fact that God *"is"* always love, theologians have invented what I like to call the "Doctrine of Schizophrenia." They teach that "God is love, but He is also judgment, and therefore, God must forever turn His back on the unrepentant sinner." Without admitting it, Christians actually agree with the words of Jonathan Edwards who, in order to justify an "eternal" hell, had to separate God's judgment from His love. To Jonathan Edwards, "hell" was the absence of the love of God. In actuality, Edwards' view of "hell" is quite correct if the Bible teaches never-ending punishments. The hypocrisy of this "schizoid" theology pits one side of God against the other instead of seeing that

God's judgments work "hand in glove" with His love in order to accomplish His purposes. Modern theology can't admit that the doctrine of "eternal" torment makes God into someone who cannot love after a man dies. At least Jonathan Edwards had the honesty (and guts) to admit what he really believed. To those reading this who believe in the doctrine of never-ending punishments – can you admit that there will come a time when God can no longer love?

The modern church embraces two gods – a god of love, and a god of judgment. This god of love can only love those who "accept" him in this life. But if a man is unfortunate enough to die at a young age without Christ, or he is born in a Muslim country, or he rejects Christianity based on the hypocrisy of so-called Christians, or he simply isn't "smart" enough to choose Christ over the thousands of sects and religions each claiming to be Truth – then look out! This god of love transforms himself into a god of judgment. No longer can this god love. No longer can he reach out to his enemies. No longer can he show any mercy or respond to the cries of those who are lost. Most of Christendom believes that this god of judgment throws most of his creation into eternal flames and then turns his back on them despite their screaming, and their cries for mercy. And this god of justice will continue to turn a deaf ear to all those people whom he created – forever and ever.

What an ugly, and hideous theology we have devised! Some men, like St. Augustine, actually claim that those who are sentenced to this never-ending torture chamber will actually be content to stay in that state for all eternity, and because of their contentment in "hell," God won't have to show His love mercy and love.

[O]f course, there is always the great theology of John Calvin who believed little innocent babies would also be tossed into the tormenting flames because they had the misfortune of being born with a sin nature.

To believe in the doctrine of "eternal" torment, one must believe one of two things about God's love. Either God stops loving those whom He throws in the lake of fire, or "eternal" torment is, in fact, God's love in action. If you believe the former, then God IS NOT love to the men He tortures; in essence you deny I John 4:8. If you believe the latter, you have changed the beautiful love of God into a sick and twisted thing – a thought so repulsive it is not even worthy of any additional discussion.

My dear friend, can you not see what a terrible lie this is? Do you really believe that God has two different personalities – one moment He acts out of love, and the next He is vengeful wrath showing no mercy and love whatsoever? Thank goodness, this is not the God of the Bible! Do we not see that God is always love? The Scriptures declare that His mercy endures forever (Psalms 136), His anger is but for a moment (Psalms 30:5), He will not cast off forever (Lamentations 3:31), He retains not His anger forever, but delights in mercy (Micah 7:18), His tender mercies are above all His works (including His judgments) (Psalms 145:9), His love never fails (I Corinthians 13:8), and above all, He is love (I John 4:8)!

To understand all the passages in the Bible that relate to God's judgments, wrath, and vengeance, we must view everything God does in the light of His love. If we understand that God does nothing apart from His love, then we understand that His judgments are but a means to bring us back to Himself (Psalms 99:8; Isaiah 4:4; 26:9). Man is incapable of being both love and justice at the same time, but the True God is both perfect love and perfect justice – at the same time! God is perfect holiness, and as such, He must deal with sin. But He is also perfect love, so anything God does must demonstrate both. We cannot separate God's justice from His love otherwise we create a schizophrenic god with two very different and contradictory personalities.

[W]hile the majority of the Church believes that God has two different personalities, we have a better testimony in the Scriptures.

"God's love will never fail!" (I Corinthians 13:8).

"Abides these three: faith, hope, and love; but the greatest is love" (I Corinthians 13:13).

We can trust that the true God of the Bible is the *"Savior of all men"* (I Timothy 4:10) and that His judgments are righteous altogether.

May all of us come to know the wondrous love that God has for ALL men – now and unto the ages of ages – and beyond!

Ken Eckerty
www.Savior-of-all.com
Niceville, FL

Appendix 25

ALL

ALL MEN

And I, if I be lifted up from the earth, will draw all men to me" (John 12:32).

"... Even so by the righteousness of One the free gift came upon all men unto justification of life" (Romans 5:18).

"Who will have all men to be saved ..." (I Timothy 2:4-6).

EVERY MAN

"That was the true Light, which lighteth every man that cometh into the world" (John 1:9).

"For as in Adam all die, even so in Christ shall all be made alive. But every man in his own order ..." (I Corinthians 15:22-23).

ALL FAMILIES

"... In thee shall all families of the earth be blessed" (Genesis 12:2-3).

ALL FLESH

"... All flesh shall see the salvation of God" (Luke 3:5-6).

ALL THE KINDREDS

"... All the kindreds of the nations shall worship before thee" (Psalm 22:27).

ALL NATIONS

"... The LORD'S house shall be established in the top of the mountains, and shall be exalted above the hills; and all nations shall flow unto it" (Isaiah 2:2).

THE WORLD

"... Behold the Lamb of God, which taketh away the sin of the world" (John 1:29).

"This is indeed the Christ, the Saviour of the world" (John 4:42).

"To wit, that God was in Christ, reconciling the world unto Himself, not imputing their trespasses unto them; and hath committed unto us the word of reconciliation" (II Corinthians 5:14, 19).

THE WHOLE WORLD

"And He is the propitiation for our sins: and not for ours only, but also for the sins of the whole world" (I John 2:2).

EVERY CREATURE

"Who is the Image of the invisible God, the Firstborn of every creature" (Colossians 1:15).

"And every creature which is in heaven, and on the earth, and under the earth, and such as are in the sea, and all that are in them, heard I saying, Blessing, and honor, and glory, and power, be unto Him that sitteth upon the throne, and unto the Lamb for ever and ever" (Revelation 5:13).

ALL THINGS

"Whom the heaven must receive until the times of restitution of all things ..." (Acts 3:21).

"For of Him, and through Him, and to Him, are all things ..." (Romans 11:36).

"And when all things shall be subdued unto Him, then shall the Son also Himself be subject unto Him that put all things under Him, that God may be all in all" (I Corinthians 15:21-28).

"That in the dispensation of the fulness of times He might gather together in one all things in Christ, both which are in heaven, and which are on earth; even in Him" (Ephesians 1:10).

"And, having made peace through the blood of His cross, by Him to reconcile all things unto Himself; by Him, I say, whether they be things in earth, or things in heaven" (Colossians 1:20).

Appendix 26

THE CASE OF JUDAS

Good were it for that man if he had not been born (Matthew 26:24; Mark 14:21).

Does this statement contradict the teaching concerning the universal reconciliation?

If it could be said of Judas that it would have been good for him if he had not been born, the inference would naturally be that Judas, at least, would not be reconciled; for, if ultimately reconciled, the blessings of that ultimate reconciliation would far outweigh the woe that he must endure as the Lord's betrayer. Therefore, notwithstanding that "woe," it would still be a good thing for him to have been born because of the ultimate blessings of reconciliation. It follows, then, that the universal reconciliation is an impossibility if this statement was really made about Judas. Did the Lord say, "Good were it for that man [Judas] if he had not been born?"

The Gospel of John does not mention this pronouncement of woe upon Judas. Luke simply records the words, *"But woe unto that man by whom He is betrayed"* (Luke 22:22). Matthew and Mark both add *"Good were it for that man if he had not been born"* (RV).

The Greek, according to the RV margin, reads, *"Good were it for **him,** if **that man** had not been born."* Who is meant by *"him"*? Who is meant by *"that man"*? *"That man"* is undoubtedly the betrayer. I would suggest that *"him"* refers to the Son of Man.

*The Son of Man goeth, even as it is written of Him, but woe unto **that man** through whom the Son of man is betrayed! Good were it for **Him** [Jesus], if **that man** [Judas] had not been born.*

The Son of Man is twice referred to by the pronoun *"Him,"* the betrayer is twice referred to by the phrase *"that man."*

Let us examine the two passages where this verse occurs.

Matthew 26:24 is part of a large passage (26:20-25), the subject of which is "The Betrayal Predicted." Its structure may be shown forth as follows:

{a} :20-21. The Betrayal Predicted.
  {b} :22. The Disciples' Query.
    {c} :23. The Lord's Answer.
{a} :24. The Betrayal Again Predicted
  {b} :25-. Judas' Query.
    {c} -:25. The Lord's Answer.

Note that :24 (designated "{a}" in the structure) is a complete member of this structure with the subject "The Betrayal Again Predicted" as its chief message.

The same is true of Mark 14:21. It is a complete member of the structure of the larger passage (Mark 14:17-21) of which the subject is "The Betrayal Predicted." The structure follows:

{a} :17-18. The Betrayal Predicted.
  {b} :19. Disciples' Query.
  {b} :20. The Lord's Answer.
{a} :21. The Betrayal Again Predicted.

Thus it is seen that Mark 14:21 (designated "{a}" in the structure) has the same subject as Matthew 26:24, "The Betrayal Again Predicted." As the wording of both verses is the same, one structure will answer for both. The structure is a simple alternative, as follows:

{a} The Son of Man

*The **Son of Man** goeth as it is written of **Him:** but woe unto that man by whom ...*

{b} The Betrayer

> ... *the son of Man is **betrayed!***

{a} The Son of Man

> *Good were it for **Him**,*

{b} The Betrayer

> ... *if **that man** had not been born.*

It might be well to note that the word translated *"good"* does not refer to essence, but to outward appearance or impression, *i.e.*, it does not mean moral goodness, but something that is beautiful, acceptable, agreeable, well-suited, pleasing.

Therefore the Son of Man was simply stating the fact that it would be acceptable or pleasing to Him if that man (the betrayer) had not been born. Why? Because then Gethsemane and Calvary could have been avoided with all their attendant agony and suffering. His soul recoiled at the thought of the Cross,

> *Now is My soul troubled; and what shall I say? Father, save Me from this hour. But for this cause came I unto this hour. Father, glorify Thy name!* (John 12:27-28).

At twelve years of age, the Lord rebuked Mary with the question, *"Knew ye not that I must be about My Father's business?"* That *"business"* included the cross.

At the beginning of His public ministry, Satan tempted Him to avoid the cross and obtain the kingdoms of the world through the worship of and submission to Satan, the Prince of this World.

In Matthew, Mark and Luke we read that in Gethsemane the Lord three times prayed,

> *My Father, if it be possible, let this cup pass away from Me: nevertheless, not as I will, but as Thou wilt.*

In His agony we read that,

His sweat became as it were great drops of blood falling down upon the ground.

In Hebrews 5:7-8 we read of Him,

Who in the days of His flesh, having offered up prayers and supplications with strong crying and tears unto Him that was able to save Him out of death, and having been heard for His godly fear, though He was a Son, yet learned He obedience by the things which He suffered.

So also in Philippians 2:8 we read that,

Being found in fashion as a man, He humbled Himself, becoming obedient even unto death, yea, the death of the cross.

He had said,

I do always the things that are pleasing to Him (John 8:29).

Again,

My meat is to do the will of Him that sent Me, and to accomplish His work (John 4:34).

Again,

Lo, I am come to do Thy will, O God (Hebrews 10:7).

God's will was the supreme thing in the Lord's life. It was His nature to be obedient to that will, even to the cross, but that obedience was put to the test again and again. Satan, at the beginning of the Lord's public ministry, urged Him to avoid the cross. Peter, towards the end of His ministry, repeated Satan's plea to avoid the sufferings of the cross. The coming of the Greeks to see the Lord Jesus suggested the thought of the coming cross and the plea, *"Father, save Me from this hour."* At the last supper this thought again intruded itself and found its expression in the words, *"acceptable* [or, pleasing] *were it for Him* [the Son of Man] *if that man* [Judas] *had not been born!"* In Gethsemane once more the battle was fought out and *"He became obedient even unto death, yea, the death of the cross."* He *"learned obedience by the things which He suffered."*

God's will even to the death on the cross, or His Own will; that which was acceptable or pleasing to God, or that which was acceptable or pleasing to Himself – which should it be? Always, amidst the sufferings that He endured as He contemplated the cross, God's will was acknowledged and obeyed. So it was when, at this last supper with His disciples, having predicted His betrayal by Judas, and the cry having been wrung from His agonized soul, *"acceptable* [or, pleasing] *were it to Him if that man had not been born."* He again crowned God's will as supreme in His life by the breaking of the bread and the passing of the cup, thereby showing that as God had decreed, so He would do. His body would be broken, His blood would be shed; for He had come to do that which was acceptable or pleasing to the Father – it was His meat to do the Father's will and to accomplish His work.

In our study of the case of Judas we have found that the Lord never said of him, *"Good were it for that man if he had not been born."* Therefore the case of Judas does not conflict with the universal reconciliation. *"Woe"* is pronounced upon him. The nature or length of that woe is not specified or even suggested.

What the Lord did not say about Judas is the negative part of our study. The positive side of that study has been centered in what He did say, namely, *"acceptable were it for Him if that man had not been born."* In that phase of our study we have received a deeper insight of our Lord's pathway of obedience, even to the death of the cross, and of the things that He suffered for us while He was choosing that which *pleased* the Father rather than that which *pleased* Himself.

H.W. Martin
Unsearchable Riches
Volume 9 (1917-1918)
Page 195

Appendix 27

My Unexpected Discovery

Chapters taken from the original edition of *My Spiritual Autobiography*
Author of *A Christian's Secret of a Happy Life* (1875)

QUESTIONINGS
(Chapter XXI)

During all the years of which I speak the Plymouth Brethren were, as I have said, among my principal teachers. But I began gradually to find some things in their teachings that I could not accept. This was especially the case with their extreme Calvinism.

There have always been, I believe, differences of opinion among them in regard of this view; but those with whom I was thrown held very rigidly the belief that some people were "elected" to salvation, and some were elected to "reprobation," and that nothing the individual could do could change these eternal decrees. We of course were among those elected to salvation, and for this we were taught to be profoundly thankful. I tried hard to fall in with this. It seemed difficult to believe that those who had taught me so much could possibly be mistaken on such a vital point. But my soul revolted from it more and more. How could I be content in knowing that I myself was sure of Heaven, when other poor souls equally deserving, but who had not had my chances, were "elected," for no fault of their own, but in the eternal decrees of God, to "Reprobation?" It seemed to me such a doctrine was utterly inconsistent with the proclamation that had so entranced me. I could not find any limitations in this proclamation, and I could not believe there were any secret limitations in the mind of the God who had made it. Neither could I see how a Creator could be just, even if He were not loving, in consigning some of the creatures He Himself, and no other, had created to the eternal torment of hell, let them be as great sinners as they might be. I felt that if this doctrine were true, I should be woefully disappointed in the God whom I had, with so much rapture, discovered.

I could not fail to see, moreover, that, after all, each of us was largely a creature of circumstance – that what we were, and what we did, was more or less the result of our temperaments, of our inherited characteristics, of our social surroundings, and of our education; and that, as these were all providentially arranged for us, with often no power on our part to alter them, it would not be just in the God who had placed us in their midst, to let them determine our eternal destiny.

As an escape from the doctrine of eternal torment, I at first embraced the doctrine of annihilation for the wicked, and for a little while tried to comfort myself with the belief that this life ended all for them. But the more I thought of it, the more it seemed to me that it would be a confession of serious failure on the part of the Creator, if He could find no way out of the problems of His creation, but to annihilate the creatures whom He had created.

Unconsciously, one of my children gave me an illustration of this. She woke me up one morning to tell me that she had been lying in bed having great fun in pretending that she had made a man. She described the color of his hair and his eyes, his figure, his height, his power, his wisdom and all the grand things he was going to do, and was very enthusiastic in her evident delight in the joy of creation. When she had finished enumerating all the magnificent qualities of her man, I said to her, "But, darling, suppose he should turn out badly; suppose he should do mischief and hurt people, and make things go wrong, what would thee do then?" "Oh," she said," I would not have any trouble; I'd just make him lie down and chop his head off."

I saw at once what a splendid illustration this was of the responsibility of a Creator, and it brought to my mind Mrs. Shelly's weird story of the artist Frankenstein, who made the monstrous image of a man, which, when it was finished, suddenly, to his horror, became alive, and went out into the world, working havoc wherever it went. The horrified maker felt obliged to follow his handiwork everywhere, in order to try to undo a little of the mischief that had been done, and to remedy as far as possible the evils it had caused. The awful sense of the responsibility that rested upon him, because of the things done by the creature he had created, opened my eyes to see the responsibility God must necessarily feel, if the creatures He had created were to turn out badly. I could not believe He would torment them forever. Neither could I rest in the thought of annihilation as His best remedy for sin. I felt hopeless of reconciling the love and the justice of the Creator with the fate of His creatures, and I knew not which way to turn. But deliverance was at hand, and the third epoch in my Christian experience was about to dawn.

THE THIRD EPOCH IN MY CHRISTIAN LIFE
(Chapter XXII)

As I stated in the last chapter, after a few years of exuberant enjoyment in the good news of salvation through Christ for myself and for those who thought as I did, my heart began to reach out after those who thought differently, and especially after those who, by reason of the providential circumstances of their birth and their surroundings, had no fair chance in life. I could not but see that ignorance of God, and, as a result, lives of sin, seemed the almost inevitable fate of a vast number of my fellow human beings, and I could not reconcile it with the justice of God, that these unfortunate mortals should be doomed to eternal torment because of those providential circumstances, for which they were not responsible, and from which, in most cases, they could not escape. The fact that I, who no more deserved it than they, should have been brought to the knowledge of the truth, while they were left out in the cold, became so burdensome to me, that I often felt as if I would gladly give up my own salvation, if by this means I could bestow it upon those who had been placed in less fortunate circumstances than myself.

I began to feel that the salvation in which I had been rejoicing was, after all a very limited and a very selfish salvation, and as such, unworthy of the Creator who had declared so emphatically that His *"tender mercies are over all His works"* (Psalm 145:9), and above all unworthy of the Lord Jesus Christ, who came into the world for the sole and single purpose of saving the world. I could not believe that His life and death for us could be meant to fall so far short of remedying the evil that He came on purpose to remedy, and I felt that it must be impossible that there could be any shortcoming in the salvation He had provided. I began to be convinced that my difficulties had simply arisen from a misunderstanding of the plans of God, and I set myself to discover the mistakes.

As I have said, my first refuge had been in the annihilation of the wicked. But this had soon seemed unworthy of a wise and good Creator and a very sad confession of failure on His part; and I could not reconcile it with either His omnipotence or His omniscience. I began to be afraid I was going to be disappointed in God. But one day a revelation came to me that vindicated Him, and that settled the whole question forever.

We very often had revivalist preachers staying with us, as we sought every opportunity of helping forward what we called "gospel work." Among the rest there came one who was very full of the idea that it was the privilege and duty of the Christian to share, in a very especial manner, in the sufferings of Christ, as well as in His joys. He seemed to think our doing so would in some way help those who knew nothing of the salvation of Christ; and he had adopted the plan of making strong appeals on the subject in his meetings, and of asking Christians, who were willing, for the sake of others, to take a share of these sufferings upon themselves, to "come forward" to a front bench in the meeting to pray that it might to granted to them. Somehow it all sounded very grand and heroic, and it fitted in so exactly with my longings to help my less fortunate fellow human beings, that, although I did not go "forward" for prayer at any of his meetings, I did begin to pray privately in a blind sort of way, that I might come into the experience, whatever it was. The result was very different from what I had expected, but it was far from tremendous.

I had expected to enter into a feeling of Christ's personal sufferings in the life and death He bore for our sakes, but instead I seemed to have a revelation, not of His sufferings because of sin, but of ours. I seemed to get a sight of the misery and anguish caused to humanity by the entrance of sin into the world, and of Christ's sorrow, not for His own sufferings because of it, but for the sufferings of the poor human beings who had been cursed by it. I seemed to understand something of what must necessarily be His anguish at the sight of the awful fate which had been permitted to befall the human race, and of His joy that He could do something to alleviate it. I saw that ours was the suffering, and that His was the joy of sacrificing Himself to save us. I felt that if I had been a Divine Creator, and had allowed such an awful fate to befall the creatures I had made, I would have been filled with anguish, and would have realized that simple justice, even if not love, required that I should find some remedy for it. And I knew I could not be more just than God. I echoed in my heart over and over again the lines found by one of George Macdonald's characters engraved on a tombstone.

> "Oh Thou, Who dist the serpent make,
> Our pardon give and pardon take."

I had been used to hearing a great deal about the awfulness of our sins against God, but now I asked myself, what about the awfulness of our fate in having been made sinners? Would I not infinitely rather that a sin should be committed against myself, than that I should commit a sin against anyone else? Was it not a far more dreadful thing to be made a sinner than to be merely sinned against? And I began to see that, since God had permitted sin to enter into the world, it must necessarily be that He would be compelled, in common fairness, to provide a remedy that would be equal to the disease. I remembered some mothers I had known, with children suffering from inherited diseases, who were only too thankful to lay down their lives in self-sacrifice for their children, if so be they might, in any way, be able to undo the harm they had done in bringing them into the world under such disastrous conditions; and I asked myself, could God do less? I saw that, when weighed in balance of wrong done, we, who had been created sinners, had infinitely more to forgive than anyone against whom we might have sinned.

The vividness with which all this came to me can never be expressed. I did not think it, or imagine it, or suppose it – I saw it. It was a revelation of the real nature of things – not according to the surface conventional ideas, but according to the actual bottom facts – and it could not be gainsaid.

In every human face I saw, there seemed to be unveiled before me the story of the misery and anguish caused by the entrance of sin into the world. I knew that God must see this with far clearer eyes than mine, and therefore I felt sure that the sufferings of this sight to Him must be infinitely beyond what it was to me, almost unbearable as that seemed. And I began to understand how it was that the least He could do would be to embrace with untold gladness anything that would help to deliver the being He had created for such awful misery.

It was a never to be forgotten insight into the world's anguish because of sin. How long it lasted I cannot remember, but, while it lasted, it almost crushed me. And as it always came afresh at the sight of a strange face, I found myself obliged to wear a thick veil whenever I went into the streets, in order that I might spare myself the awful realization.

One day I was riding on a tramcar along Market Street, Philadelphia, when I saw two men come in and seat themselves opposite to me. I saw them dimly through my veil, but congratulated myself that it was only dimly, as I was thus spared the wave of anguish that had so often swept over me at the full sight of a strange face. The conductor came for his fare, and I was obliged to raise my veil in order to count it out. As I raised it I got a sight of the faces of those two men, and with an overwhelming flood of anguish, I seemed to catch a fresh and clearer revelation of the depth of the misery that had been caused to human beings by sin. It was more than I could bear. I clenched my hands and cried out in my soul, "O, God, how canst thou bear it? Thou mightest have prevented it, but didst not. Thou mightest even now change it, but Thou dost not. I do not see how Thou canst go on living, and endure it." I upbraided God. And I felt I was justified in doing so. Then suddenly God seemed to answer me. An inward voice said, in tones of infinite love and tenderness, *"He shall see of the travail of His soul and be satisfied"* (Isaiah 53:11). "Satisfied!" I cried in my heart, "Christ is to be satisfied! He will be able to look at the world's misery, and then at the travail through which He has passed because of it, and will be satisfied with the result. If I were Christ, nothing could satisfy me but that every human being should in the end be saved, and therefore I am sure that nothing less will satisfy Him." And with this a veil seemed to be withdrawn from before the plans of the universe, and I saw that it was true, as the Bible says, that *"as in Adam all die even so in Christ should all be made alive"* (I Corinthians 15:22). As was the first, even so was the second. The *"all"* in one case could not in fairness mean less than the *"all"* in the other. I saw therefore that the remedy must necessarily be equal to the disease. The salvation must be as universal as the fall.

I saw all this that day on the tramcar on Market Street, Philadelphia – not only thought it, or hoped it, or even believed it, but knew it. It was a Divine fact. And from that moment I have never had one questioning thought as to the final destiny of the human race. God is the Creator of every human being, therefore He is the Father of each one, and they are all His children; and Christ died for every one, and is declared to be *"the propitiation not for our sins only, but also for the sins of the whole world"* (I John 2:2). However great the ignorance therefore, or however grievous the sin, the promise of salvation is positive and without limitations. If it is true that *"by the offense of one judgement came upon all men to condemnation,"* it is equally true that *"by the righteousness of one the free gift came upon all men unto justification of life"* (Romans 5:18). To limit the last *"all men"* is also to limit the first. The salvation is absolutely equal to the fall. There is to be a final *"restitution of all things"* (Acts 3:21; *c.f.* I Corinthians 15:28), when *"at the name of Jesus every knee shall bow, of things in heaven, and things on earth, and things under the earth, and every tongue shall confess that Jesus Christ is Lord to the glory of God the Father"* (Philippians 2:10). Every knee, every tongue – words could not be more embracing. The how and when I could not see; but the one essential fact was all I needed: somewhere and somehow God was going to make every thing right for all the creatures He had created. My heart was at rest about it forever.

I hurried home to get hold of my Bible, to see if the magnificent fact I had discovered could possibly have been all this time in the Bible, and I had not seen it. The moment I entered the house, I did not wait to take off my bonnet, but rushed at once to the table where I always kept my Bible and Concordance ready for use, and began my search. Immediately the whole Book seemed to be illuminated. On every page the truth concerning the *"times of restitution of all things"* (Acts 3:21) of which the Apostle Peter says *"God Has spoken by the mouth of all His holy prophets since the world began,"* shone forth, and no room was left for questioning. I turned greedily from page to page of my Bible, fairly laughing aloud for joy at the blaze of light that illuminated it all. It became a new book. Another skin seemed to have been peeled off every text, and my Bible fairly shone with a new meaning. I do not say with a different meaning, for in no sense did the new meaning contradict the old, but a deeper meaning, the true meaning, hidden behind the outward form of words. The words did not need to be changed, they only needed to be understood; and now at last I began to understand them.

I remember just about this time, in the course of my daily reading in the Bible, coming to the Psalms, and I was amazed at the new light thrown upon their apparently most severe and bloodthirsty denunciations. I saw that, when rightly interpreted, not by the letter, but by the spirit, they were full of the assured and final triumph of good over evil, and were a magnificent vindication of the goodness and justice of God, who will not, and ought not, and cannot, rest until all His enemies and ours are put under His feet. I saw that the kingdom must be interior before it can be exterior, that it is a kingdom of ideas, and not one of brute force; that His rule is over hearts, not over places; that His victories must be inward before they can be outward; that He seeks to control spirits rather than bodies; that no triumph could satisfy Him but a triumph that gains the heart; that in short, where God really reigns, the surrender must be the interior surrender of the convicted free men, and not merely the outward surrender of the conquered slave. Milton says, "Who overcomes by force hath overcome but half his foe," and I saw that this was true.

Read in the light of these views, my whole soul thrilled with praise over the very words that had before caused me to thrill with horror: *"Let God arise, let His enemies be scattered; let them also that hate Him flee before Him. As smoke is driven away, so drive them away: as wax melted before the fire, so let the wicked perish at the presence of God"* (Psalm 68:1-2). God's wrath is against the sin, not against the sinner, and when His enemies are scattered, ours are also. His sword is the righteousness that puts to death sin in order to save the sinner. The fire of His anger is the "refiner's fire," and He sits, not as the destroyer of the human soul, but as its purifier, to purge it as gold and silver are purged.

Implacable is love
Foes may be bought or teased
From their malign intent;
But He goes unappeased
Who is on kindness bent.

The Psalmist says, *"You were a God Who forgave **them,** though You take vengeance of **their inventions"*** (Psalm 99:8); and with this key to interpret it, all the denunciations of God's wrath, which had once seemed so cruel and so unjust, were transformed into declarations of His loving determination to make us good enough to live in Heaven with Himself forever.

I might multiply endlessly similar instances of the new illumination that shone in entrancing beauty on every page of the Bible, but these will suffice. I began at last to understand what the Apostle Paul meant when he said that he had been made the minister of the New Testament, not of the letter but of the spirit, for *"the letter kills but the spirit gives life"*(II Corinthians 3:6). Things I had read in the letter, and had shuddered at, now, read in the spirit, filled me with joy.

THE UNSELFISHNESS OF GOD
(CHAPTER XXIII)

I have always felt that this time my real discovery of the unselfishness of God began. Up to then, while I had rejoiced in the salvation for myself that I had discovered, I had been secretly beset from time to time with a torturing feeling that, after all, it was rather a selfish salvation, both for Him and for me. How could a good God enjoy Himself in Heaven, knowing all the while that a large proportion of the beings He had Himself created were doomed to eternal misery, unless He were a selfish God? I had known that the Bible said that He was a God of love, and I had supposed that it must be true, but always there had been at the bottom of my mind this secret feeling that His love could not stand the test of comparison with the ideal of love in my own heart. I knew that, poor and imperfect as my love must be, I could never have enjoyed myself in Heaven while one of my children, no matter how naughty, was shut out; and, that He could and did enjoy Himself, while countless thousands of His children were shut out, seemed to me a failure in the most essential element of love. So that, grateful as I had felt for the blessings of forgiveness and of a sure and certain hope of Heaven for myself, I still had often felt as if after all the God I worshiped was a selfish God, Who cared more for His Own comfort and His Own glory than He did for the poor suffering beings He had made. But now I began to see that the wideness of God's love was far beyond any wideness that I could even conceive of; and that if I took all the unselfish love of every mother's heart the whole world over, and piled it all together, and multiplied it by millions, I would still only get a faint idea of the unselfishness of God.

I had always thought of Him as loving, but now I found out that He was far more than loving: He was love, love embodied and ingrained. I saw that He was, as it were, made out of love, so that in the very nature of things He could not do anything contrary to love. Not that He would not do it, but actually could not, because love was the very essence of His being. I saw that the law of love, like the law of gravitation, is inevitable in its working, and that God is, if I may say so, under this law, and cannot help obeying it. I saw that, because He is love, He simply, in the very nature of things, must be loving. It is not a matter of choice with Him, but a matter of necessity. I saw that, once this fact was known, to trust in this God of love would be as natural as to breathe. Every doubting question was answered, and I was filled with an illimitable delight in the thought of having been created by such an unselfish God. I saw that as a matter of course the fact of His being our creator was an absolute guarantee that He would care for us, and would make all things work together for our good. The duties of ownership blazed with tremendous illumination. Not its rights, of which I had hitherto chiefly thought, but its duties, the things ownership necessarily demands of its owner. I saw that just as in a civilized community people are compelled by public opinion, or if necessary by the law, to take proper care of things that belong to them, so our Creator, by the laws of common morality, is compelled to take proper care of the creatures He has created, and must be held responsible for their well being.

It was all so glorious that it often seemed too good to be true, that we actually did belong to such an unselfish God; that many a time, when a fresh insight into His goodness would come over me, I would be obliged to get my Bible and open it at the texts that declared we really were His property, and put my fingers on them, and read them aloud, just to reassure myself that they did actually say, without any limitations, that He was my owner.

The expression *"Remember your Creator"* (Ecclesiastics 12:1) assumed a totally different aspect to me. I had always thought of it as a kind of threat held over us into good behavior; but now it seemed full of the most delightful warrant and assurance that all was well for the creatures this unselfish Creator had created. I saw that God was good, not religiously good only, but really and actually good in the truest sense of the word, and that a good Creator was of course bound to make every thing go right with the creatures He had created. The fact that nothing was hid from His eyes, which had once been so alarming, now began to seem the most delightful fact in the whole universe, because it made it certain that He knew all about us, and would therefore be able to do His best for us.

My own feelings as a mother, which had heretofore seemed to war with what I had believed of God, now came into perfect harmony.

My children have been the joy of my life. I cannot imagine more exquisite bliss than comes to one sometimes in the possession and companionship of a child. To me there have been moments, when my arms have been around my children, that have seemed more like what the bliss of Heaven must be than any other thing I can conceive of; and I think this feeling has taught me more of what are God's feelings towards His children than anything else in the universe. If I, a human being with limited capacity, can find such joy in my children, what must God, with His infinite heart of love, feel towards His? In fact most of my ideas of the love and goodness of God have come from my own experience as a mother, because I could not conceive that God would create me with a greater capacity for unselfishness and self sacrifice than He possessed Himself. Since this discovery of the mother heart of God I have always been able to answer every doubt that may have arisen in my mind, as to the extent and quality of the love of God, by simply looking at my own feelings as a mother. I cannot understand the possibility of any selfishness on the mother's part coming into her relation to her children. It seems to me a mother, who can be selfish and think of her own comfort and her own welfare before that of her children, is an abnormal mother, who fails in the very highest duty of motherhood.

If one looks at what we call the lower creation, one will see that every animal teaches us this supreme duty of self-sacrifice on the part of the mother.

The tiger mother will suffer herself to be killed rather than that that harm should come to her offspring. She will starve that they may have food. Could our God do less? I speak of self-sacrifice, but I cannot truthfully call it sacrifice. Any true mother, who knows the reality of motherhood, would scorn the idea that the care of her children involved a sacrifice, in the ordinary sense of sacrifice, on her part. It may involve trouble or weariness, but not what I could call sacrifice. The sacrifice would be if she were not allowed to care for them, not if she were. I know no more fallacious line of argument than that which is founded upon the idea that children ought to be grateful for the self-sacrifice on the mother's part. Her claim to love and consideration on the part of her children depends altogether to my mind upon how true a mother she has been in the sense I describe; and I believe that thousands of disappointed mothers, who have not received the gratitude and consideration they would like, have only themselves to thank, because they have demanded it, instead of having won it. All this has taught me to understand God's feelings towards us: that what we call self-sacrifice on the part of Christ was simply the absolutely necessary expression of His love for us; and that the amazing thing would have been, not that He did it, but if He had not done it.

Since I had this insight of the mother-heart of God, I have never been able to feel the slightest anxiety for any of His children; and by His children I do not mean only the good ones, but I mean the bad ones just as much. Are we not distinctly told that the Good Shepherd leaves the ninety and nine good sheep in order to find the one naughty sheep that is lost, and that He looks for it until He finds it? Viewed in the light of motherhood, has not that word "*lost*" a most comforting meaning, since nothing can be lost that is not owned by somebody, and to be lost means only not yet found? The lost gold piece is still gold, with the image of the King upon it; the lost sheep is a sheep still, not a wolf; the lost son has still the blood of his father in his veins.

Thus if a person is a lost sinner, it only means that he is owned by the Good Shepherd, and that the Good Shepherd is bound, by the very duties of His ownership, to go after that which is lost, and to go until He finds it. The word "*lost*" therefore, to my mind, contains in itself the strongest proof of ownership that one could desire. Who can imagine a mother with a lost child ever having a ray of comfort until the child is found, and who can imagine a God being more indifferent than a mother? In fact I believe that all the problems of the spiritual life, which are often so distressing to conscientious souls, would vanish like mist before the rising sun, if the full blaze of the mother-heart of God should be turned upon them.

Moreover, I saw that since it was declared we were created in the image of God, we were bound to believe that the best in us, and not the worst, was the reflection of that image, and that therefore things which to us in our best moments looked selfish, or unkind, or unjust, or self-seeking, must never, no matter what the "seeming," be attributed to God. If He is unselfish, He must be at least as unselfish as the highest human ideal; and of course we know He must be infinitely more.

All the texts in the Bible revealing God's goodness shone with a new meaning, and I saw that His goodness was not merely a patronizing benevolence, but was a genuine *bona fide* goodness that included unselfishness and consideration, and above all justice, which last has always seemed to me one of the very first elements of goodness. No unjust person could ever, in my opinion, lay the slightest claim to being good, let their outward seemings of goodness be as deceiving as they may. I had in short such an overwhelming revelation of the intrinsic and inherent goodness and unselfishness of God that nothing since has been able to shake it. A great many things in His dealings have been and still are mysteries to me; but I am sure they could all be explained on the basis of love and justice, if only I could look deep enough; and that some day I shall see, what now I firmly believe, that His loving kindness is really and truly over all His works.

I do not mean to say that all this acquaintance with God came to me at once; but I do mean to say that when I had that revelation on the tram-car in Philadelphia that day, a light on the character of God began to shine, that has never since waned in the slightest, and has only grown brighter and brighter with every year of my life. It is enough for me to say "God is" and I have the answer to every possible difficulty.

The amazing thing is that I, in company with so many other Christians, had failed, with the open Bible before me, to see this; and that all sorts of travesties on the character of God, and of libels upon His goodness, can find apparently a welcome entrance into Christian hearts. To me such things became at this time well nigh intolerable. I could listen patiently, and even with interest, to any sort of strange or heretical ideas that did not touch the character of God, but the one thing I could not endure, and could not sit still to listen to, was anything that contained, even under a show of great piety, the least hint of a libel on His love or His selfishness.

I shall never forget a memorable occasion in our own house, when a celebrated Preacher from Boston, was visiting us. The conversation at the breakfast table turned on the subject of God's love, and this Preacher declared that you must not count on it too much, as there were limits as to what His love could endure, just as there were limits to a mother's love; and he went on to declare that there were certain sins a daughter could commit which the mother never could forgive, and which would forever close her heart and her home against her child, and he asserted that it was just so with God, and that he considered it was a grandmotherly religion that taught anything different.

I have no doubt his object was to combat my views on Restitution, although we were not talking on that subject; but he evidently wanted to convince me that God was not quite so foolishly loving as I thought. It was more than I could endure to hear both mothers, and the God who made mothers, so maligned, and, although the speaker was my guest, I broke forth into a perfect passion of indignation, and, declaring that I would not sit at the table with any one who held such libelous ideas of God, I burst into tears and left the room, and entirely declined to see my guest again. I do not say this was right or courteous, or at all Christ-like, but it only illustrates how overwhelmingly I felt on the subject. The honor of God seemed to me of more importance than any ordinary rules of politeness. But I see now that I might have vindicated that honor in an equally effectual but more Christ-like way.

Still, to this day, the one thing which I find it very hard to tolerate, is any thing which libels the character of God. Nothing else matters like this, for all our salvation depends wholly and entirely upon what God is; and unless He can be proved to be absolutely good, and absolutely unselfish, and absolutely just, our case is absolutely hopeless. God is our salvation, and, if He fails us, in even the slightest degree, we have nowhere else to turn.

Hannah Whitall Smith (1832-1911)

Appendix 28

GOD'S VAST LOVE

Most thinking is fathered by a wish and mothered by a fear. It is well, therefore, to look to our ruling desires and dominant fears if we would escape the natural prejudices which warp our thinking. This is true in respect to strictly mundane matters where we, in some measure, know our way around. Yet it is more notably the case in spiritual things, where we could know nothing at all except by revelation; and if our concepts of revelation are warped by pagan philosophy, we shall understand God's purposes but poorly, indeed.

Paul, God's mouthpiece to the Gentiles, says on this point:

Now the soulish man is not receiving the things which are of the spirit of God, for they are stupidity to him, and he is not able to know them, seeing that they are spiritually examined (I Corinthians 2:14).

A *"soulish"* man is simply one who relies on his senses to guide him in his concepts of what God is like and of what He intends to do to and for the human race.

Would we show much love for our human friends if we never read the letters they take the trouble to write us about what they intend to do; or if we read them so superficially or with such cock-sureness of what we think they are going to say that what they do say makes no impression? Yet we do those very things with God's Word.

He says: *"In Christ all shall be vivified"* (I Corinthians 15:22), and we say, "Oh no: that means He is going to make some dead."

He says He is going to *"head up all in the Christ – both that in the heavens and that on the earth"* (Ephesians 1:10), and we say, "He will certainly scatter part of it."

When God gives us a glimpse into His purpose to *"reconcile all to Him"* (Colossians 1:20), we object that He will forever antagonize some. We just know better than God does, that's all.

When God's Word tells us that God is to be *"All in all"* (I Corinthians 15:28), our prejudices tell us that He means only "All in some." We feel that God is not even God over all, to say nothing of being God in all. The majestic human will must be glorified at any cost.

But let's have done with human feelings as a guide to divine revelation. Our feelings vary greatly, often affected by the most trivial circumstances.

"That which the eye did not perceive, and the ear did not hear, and to which the heart of man did not ascend whatever, God makes ready for those who are loving Him" – that which could not be known by sensuous perception, *"to us God reveals them through His spirit"* (I Corinthians 2:9-10).

There you are: follow your natural judgment and miss the truth; give heed to the Word of God and have a wisdom which comes from no other source. It all depends on what you want: divine truth or self flattery. The two things will not stay in the same heart at the same time.

When we read of the living God being *"the Savior of all mankind"* (I Timothy 4:10); when we learn that the Son of Man shall draw all to Himself (John 12:32) as the universal center of gravity; when it is made plain to us that God our Savior *"wills that all mankind be saved and come into a realization of the truth"* (I Timothy 2:4), and that Christ Jesus is the One giving Himself *"a correspondent Ransom for all"* (I Timothy 2:6) – the same *"all"* that God wills to be saved (2:4) and for whom believers should pray (2:1); when God's benevolent determination to be *"annulling the acts of the Adversary"* (I John 3:8) is revealed to us; when we are informed that death, being the *"last enemy,"* will be abolished (I Corinthians 15:26), we as believers have no course open to us but to believe.

These are matters concerning which we could know nothing except as God tells us; and this is what God has told us. The slight difficulties which suggest themselves are practically all traceable to the presence of ecclesiastical philosophy in our minds or to faults in our English translations of the Sacred Scriptures.

God's Word, being true, makes every man who does not speak in accord with it a liar (Romans 3:4).

> But men make His love too narrow
>   By false limits of their own,
> And they magnify His justice
>   With a zeal He will not own.
>
> For the love of God is broader
>   Than the measure of man's mind;
> And the heart of our Creator
>   Is most wonderfully kind.

One reason, probably the principal reason, why we are so slow to believe in the kindness of God's heart is our innate subconsciousness of sin and its attendant fear of the consequences; and there is no way to escape this fear except by repose in what God in Christ has done to rescue us. There is no place to hear what God has done except in His Word, for *"faith is out of tidings, yet tidings through a declaration of Christ"* (Romans 10:17).

Mind: our worst fears about sin and its deserts are well founded; and all that pagan religions (in whatever land) have done is to chafe the sore that is already there; all that human ethics and philosophies have done is to try to get people to forget without any authoritative ground for forgetting. All that pleasure seekers and jazz makers can do is to occupy the attention, to keep it away from the thought of sin.

Yet the honest truth is we are in a bad way unless God has done something about it. The pertinent question is, "Did Christ appear in order to put away sin once for all by the sacrifice of Himself?" (Hebrews 9:26). If He did, the penalty not only was paid but *is* paid; and no one can be asked to suffer pain of any pitch, intensity or duration as a penalty, or be called upon to "satisfy" a justice which Christ Himself has already fully vindicated. Is the grace, the undeserved kindness of God to be thus frustrated by human additions? *"Not by me,"* says Paul (Galatians 2:21).

Furthermore, is Christ Jesus, having begun the good work, unable to bring it to completion? Is He unable to cope with sin so that it will never cease to be? Is the law and its death penalty to exist when death is abolished? Are there to be tortured or even dead enemies when all things in heaven and earth are reconciled to God – brought into grateful, friendly appreciation of His loving kindness? Is God, with all power and wisdom concentrated in His risen Son, unable to bring to bear influences which will affect the motives, the inmost preferences of every individual, as He did with Abel, with Saul of Tarsus, and with every one of us who believe? Is not Christ the *"power of God"* as well as the *"wisdom of God"* (I Corinthians 1:24)?

What say the Scriptures?

> I John 3:4 – Sin is lawlessness.

> Romans 3:20 – Through law is the recognition of sin.

> Romans 7:8 – Apart from law sin is dead.

Sin, as a judicial technicality, is thus identified with laws; but what has been actually done about it?

> Galatians 3:13 – Christ reclaims us from the curse of the law, becoming a curse for our sakes.

> John 1:29 – Lo! the Lamb of God Which is taking away the sin of the world!

> Hebrews 9:26 – Since then, He must often be suffering from the disruption of the world, yet now, once, at the conclusion of the eons, for the repudiation of sin through His sacrifice, is He manifest.

> II Corinthians 5:19 – Not reckoning their offenses to them.

> II Peter 2:24 – Who Himself carries up our sins in His body on to the pole.

Is the mighty Maker so poor a workman that He will have to discard the most of His work? Or will He gather up the fragments so that nothing will be lost? What humanly conducted factory could rate for efficiency if it had to dump most, or even much of its product into some hellhole or offal place of perdition?

Of course there are parables and other statements, most of them applying to Christ's thousand-year reign as the Son of Man, or to the immediate preparation for that reign, which speak in a different tone. **Right here it is well to note that the greatest single cause of confusion in Scripture study consists in failure to discern correctly the times, seasons, dispensations, classes, etc., which are in God's plan.**

The thousand-year reign of Christ, often called the millennium, is something of a reversion, in that it goes back to law. It gives men the flawless rule, the righteous government which they think they need to have a fair "chance." It is given to them to prove that they need something more. The present dispensation, however, is one in which grace reigns and not law (Romans 5:21). The same will be true in the eon to follow the millennium, although even the judgments of Christ's reign are disciplinary rather than penal; for when the Lamb of God bore away the sin of the world, He bore it all away – not our sins up to date with a running account thereafter, which would benefit us none, seeing we were born after His sacrifice was made.

No act of sin is now or will ever be the cause of condemnatory sentence or of penal suffering on the part of anybody. Thank God for that. There is discipline, however; but what a difference to the heart of faith!

> *For the love of Christ is constraining us, judging this, that, if one died for the sake of all, consequently all died. And He died for the sake of all that those who are living should by no means still be living to themselves, but to the One dying and being roused for their sakes.*

The dying is finished. Sin is dealt with in its judicial aspects, though we still experience it for discipline of faith until our change comes (Philippians 3:20, 21). The almighty Head of the New Creation is dealing now principally with ignorance and unbelief. These obscure the light of the glory of God as it shines in the face of Jesus Christ no less than sin.

Only a sense of one's own insufficiency-without-God-and-His-Christ can bring one to trust in that God and Christ. The churches are full of indoctrinated unbelievers. As long as they think they are self-sufficient, in unit or in group, they are going to stay unbelievers, no matter what they know; because faith is trust in a Person. Until they can sing with sincerity, as well as with truth, "nothing in my hand I bring," there will be no reconciliation, no lively appreciation of the fact that **His will is sweeter than our wish.**

Saul of Tarsus was certainly no small sinner, "foremost representative" he calls himself (I Timothy 1:15); he was ignorant and unbelieving (I Timothy 1:13); yet we see how the grace of God was shown to him. He was a calumniator, a persecutor, and an outrager or brutal person in his persecutions. It would be difficult to find a harder case; but one glimpse of his glorified Lord and that stony heart was melted down like butter. One word from that gracious voice, which spoke as never man spoke, and his ignorance of God as He is began to be dispelled. A few words from a heaven-sent and heaven-instructed brother, and unbelief dissolved like discontent on the bosom of a great calm.

"Who art Thou?" was his cry. "I am justice, whom thou disregardest" did the glorious One say? Not being taught by the Pharisees, He did not. "I am Jesus Savior!" How different. Not a condemner but a rescuer. The wrong-doer was arrested by love, and there broken, contrite he lay at the feet of his risen Lord.

All this, Paul tells us, was in the nature of a pattern of what God intended to do to and for other unbelievers who were to come to believe.

> Therefore was I shown mercy, that in me, the foremost [sinner], Jesus Christ should be displaying all His patience, for a pattern of those who are about to be believing on Him for life eonian (I Timothy 1:16).

Saul was not punished for his iniquity. The One Whom he persecuted had already paid the penalty for the sin of persecution in Saul. There was no penalty, but much discipline. There is not only no future punishment for sin but no punishment now. "Sin reigns in death" only (Romans 5:21). Sin has no resurrection. In the death of Christ sin came to an end and in the resurrection power of Christ "grace reigns through righteousness," superabundant above sin and its consequences by virtue of the headship of Jesus Christ our Lord.

Man's dread of a hell of torment is taught by the precepts of men, not by the Word of God. Read Romans 6:1-14 and see how simply the apostle presents the facts. Our horizon has been entirely filled by sin and sinners. It is like moaning over a debt that's paid. Christ, not sin, should have the preeminence in all things.

And know this: **No sin however heinous, and no aggregation of sinners, however numerous or ignorant or willful, can bankrupt the riches of God's grace or undo what was done on Calvary's brow.** If peace is not made by the blood of His cross then it will not be made by any effort or righteousness of our own.

Now thanks be to God, Who always gives us a triumph in Christ!

Since mine eyes were fixed on Jesus
    I've lost sight of all beside
So enchained my spirit's vision
    Looking at the Crucified

E.H. Robison (1885-1932)

(See also the author's *Christ and Religion* that ran in BSN #183.)

Fredrik H. Robison had an interesting journey to the truth. He served as personal secretary to Charles Taze Russell, founder of *The Watch Tower Bible & Tract Society*. In 1909 he was given oversight of the Watchtower's foreign operations and was a member of the five-man editorial committee of *The Watch Tower,* responsible for approving each and every article appearing in its columns. In 1918 he was one of the *Watchtower* officials charged with governmental sedition and sentenced to Federal prison. In 1922 his understanding of Scripture changed and he left *The Watchtower Bible & Tract Society* to successfully follow his conscience. Robison conducted independent Bible studies on the life and epistles of Paul in Washington, D.C., sponsored by some of his friends. He eventually authored very helpful articles (including this one: *God's Vast Love*) that appeared in *Unsearchable Riches* magazine, and also wrote *Are Bride and Body Identical?* published by the *Concordant Publishing Concern.*

Appendix 29

WHO ARE YOU?

and What Have You Done with My Real Father?

People can only fully and accurately understand what they are capable of relating to by experience. Without experience, one may be able to answer the question of how something happens, but true understanding is more firmly hinged upon **why** something happens. Experience brings understanding that classes, quizzes, tests and reading cannot. I may understand how Christ died for my sins by reading about it in the Bible; I may even grasp the fact that Christ's sacrifice was done out of love, but only after seeing and feeling His love and loving as He did do I understand **why** He died. Only after loving someone enough to sacrifice myself for them can I relate to even the smallest part of the love that God had for the world when He gave His Son for it. After experiencing the bond between a father and a son and after understanding that unconditional love which would cause me to continue to give my life for my father over and over again forever, I can finally begin to grasp how much I would have to love the world to will my only father's suffering and death to save the world. Theologians, scholars, priests, preachers and men of the cloth can talk about eternal conscious torment until they turn blue, but my answer to their depiction of a Father who would torture His children forever will always be "That's not my God!"

Yes, it is true. I proudly and loudly proclaim it. If the God Whom others worship has a nature which absolutely negates love, that God is not my God. The God I worship goes by the name "Love" and *"Savior of all men."* In today's version of Christianity, worshiping and sucking up to a god who finds pleasure in burning his children alive forever is the only way to get on his good side and spare one's own well-being. If my father told me to serve him faithfully and lovingly while he burned my sisters alive forever; my response would not be "Hooray! Such good news!" Rather, it would be, "Who are you and what have you done with my **real** father?" So should be the response of every Christian when they hear the doctrine of eternal conscious torment.

The idea of all men receiving eternal life is thought to be heretical by partialists, but even partialists believe that all will have eternal life. They may not realize this because the idea of a man living in death is so ridiculously contradictory, but partialists believe that *every* man will have eternal life; only most of these will live eternally in a "place" called death. Partialists claim that the inhabitants of *"the second death"* are alive; and not just alive for a period of time until they die, but alive forever. The very thought of this may sound silly, but over a billion people on the planet right now hold more strongly to this teaching than they do to the teaching that two plus two equals four. Unfortunately for them, anyone who does not loudly proclaim "take my brain, just don't take my religion" is immediately labeled as a heretic by the chairmen of each and every organized religion on the planet. Partialists also claim to believe that the last enemy which will be destroyed is death (I Corinthians 15:26), however they deny this belief with the contradictory belief that *"the second death"* is never-ending.

So, why did God put us here? Is our existence the result of an accident that God didn't see coming 6,000 years ago, or is our existence and our experience in this life part of God's plan? Scripture is clear about the fact that God had a plan before the foundation of the world, but was that plan foiled after Adam and Eve sinned? All these questions have one simple answer. Why are we here? God willed it so. Why are we going through this experience in our short life here? God willed it so. God's plan was not foiled by sin. He was not surprised to see sin come into the equation. God is the potter, we are the clay and our life full of experiences here is the means by which God molds us. I am not saying that God is actively dragging each of us through certain experiences; I am saying that each person's life consists of experiences caused by decisions and situations we face and that we are molded regardless of whether we choose sin or righteousness.

Take Paul's experiences for example. Was Paul's life affected by sin? Sure, he tempted and was tempted, he betrayed and was betrayed, he hated and was hated, he killed and was killed. Did Paul suffer? Absolutely. Did Paul have the opportunity not to walk with God? Yes. In the end, Paul chose righteousness instead of sin and he was molded by his experiences. Now consider Pharaoh's life. Was Pharaoh's life affected by sin? Sure, he tempted and was tempted, he betrayed and was betrayed, he hated and was hated, he killed and was killed. Did Pharaoh suffer? Absolutely. Did Pharaoh have the opportunity not to walk with God? Yes. In the end, Pharaoh chose sin instead of righteousness and he was molded by his experiences. In Pharaoh's case, his heart was hardened by God to fulfill God's plan (Exodus 7:13), and in Paul's case, his heart was softened by God on the road to Damascus. Both of these men were not only molded directly by God, but molded indirectly by God through their experiences and contact with a sin-cursed world.

Will Paul be rewarded without end by God because God chose to soften Paul's heart, but Pharaoh will be tormented without end by God because God chose to harden Pharaoh's heart? Or can we submit the fact that God's will is supreme over ours? Are our sin-cursed experiences here an accident by God – a result of God's apparent lack of foresight – or were we put here by God on purpose after the counsel of His own will which Ephesians 1:11 depicts as a higher authority than man's stubbornness? Will death someday be destroyed and life given to all who were dead (the only way to destroy death is with life)? Or will/can non-believers be dead and alive at the same time for all time? I subscribe to the belief that God will accomplish what He planned, even if the rest of the Christian world finds God's will to be impractical and undoable.

Aaron Locker

Appendix 30

TO THE BEST OF HIS ABILITY

When I was in high school, my principal did not measure the performance of one student against the performance of another. He knew that different people were good at different things. He would say, "I want you to do your school work to the best of your ability." A student who was very capable in science but had trouble understanding math was never expected to perform in math the same as a student who was very capable in math. If a student worked to the best of their ability and got all B's on their report card, they were congratulated for their hard work, not frowned upon because they didn't get any A's.

Working to the best of one's ability is a concept that is rooted deeply into creation by the Creator. God would have us to work hard at things, not to be lazy. This concept is shown in Jesus's "parable of the talents" in Matthew 25:15. The lord of the servants gave five talents to one servant, two talents to another servant and finally one talent to a third servant. The lord didn't do this because he favored one servant over another, but, as verse 15 shows, he gave *"to every man according to his several ability."* When the lord returned, the first two servants had performed to the best of their ability, but the third servant did not. The lord was displeased with the servant that did not perform to the best of his ability.

We have a God who is infinitely capable to do everything He pleases. While every Christian I have ever talked to would admit this, they refuse to believe that our God would work to the best of His ability to accomplish what He wills. In fact, most Christians believe that while it is God's will to see all men saved (I Timothy 2:4), and it is contrary to God's will to see any perish (Matthew 18:15), that God will accomplish abundantly more against His will than He will accomplish for His will. If the almighty Creator of the universe will, in the end, be farther from His goal than He was in the beginning, as the Arminians teach, how foolish it would be for man, who can accomplish nothing without God, to put any energy at all into working after God's will. If the all-powerful God will be exceedingly counterproductive in accomplishing His will, any attempt by man to accomplish God's will can be nothing but pure evil.

I hope, in the future, to see more Christians embrace a God who works to the best of His infinite ability to accomplish the good pleasure of His will; and that when they hear a strange doctrine like that of eternal conscious torment which is entirely uncharacteristic of God, they will not hold fast to their belief of eternal conscious torment simply because it is what they, or their preacher, have always believed, but will discard their bias and search the Scripture to see what it says on the matter. Let it not be so important to ask, "Do you believe in God?" but to ask instead, "Who is the God in Whom you believe?" For if the nature of one's God is anger, frustration and inability, I submit that it may be better to believe in no God at all than to worship a monster who makes Adolf Hitler look like a generous man.

Aaron Locker

WHICH IS BETTER?

Which Is Better?

A God Who *saves:*

some
many
all

A God Who:

annihilates some people
punishes some people
restores all people to Him

A God Whose *will* is:

limited
unlimited

A God Whose *power* is:

limited
unlimited

A God Whose *love* is:

limited
unlimited

A God Whose *compassion* is:

limited
unlimited

A God Who has *reconciled:*

some
many
all

A God Who:

    does impute sin
    does not impute sin

A God Whose *mercy* is:

    limited
    unlimited

A God Who:

    hates His enemies
    loves His enemies

A God Whose *grace* is:

    limited
    unlimited

A God Who has created an endless:

    Hell
    Hope

A God Who includes:

    some
    many
    all

A God Who depends on:

    my faith
    His faith

A God Who:

    is limited by man's will
    has absolute sovereignty

Which Is Best?

Depending on how you answered these questions, you end up with an image of God that is either *limited* or *unlimited*.

Which is *best*?

    a *limited* God?
    an *unlimited* God?

What do *you choose* to believe about God?

    God is *limited*.
    God is *unlimited*.

Which would be more honoring to God?

Believe the Best!

If you prefer the best wouldn't you think that God would also? For God to prefer the best He would use all things He has made in His Wisdom. God's best would bring all creation to a desired end or goal accomplishing His purpose.

Doesn't this bring peace of mind, harmony, joy and satisfaction with no condemnation?

He corrects and caresses us into His image. In this "best" view of God, there are no worries, threats, or fears. His generosity is for all and to all. The God of all creation is all knowing and all powerful. His plan, purpose, and pleasure shall be done.

Isn't this better than a limited God? Wouldn't you prefer this better understanding of God? Truth makes all people free. Share these questions with others. They will challenge their thinking and understanding of The Almighty God.

Our view of God determines how we live our lives. Our view of God determines how we treat other people, as individuals or as groups.

THE SLANDER OF GOD

Don't believe the slander about God. The nature and character of God has been shamefully maligned for centuries. His image has been perverted into a "god" who either cannot or will not carry out His desired purposes.

Don't believe in a "god":

Who loves man ...

> *but gives up most of them to endless torture.*

Who sent His Son to make the payment of sin for every man ...

> *but makes most men pay for their own sins.*

Who allowed mankind to fall into sin in the Garden of Eden ...

> *with full knowledge that in the end He would not be able to redeem most of them.*

Who wants all men to be saved ...

> *but will damn most of them.*

Who tells us to love and do good to our enemies ...

while He torments His enemies endlessly.

This is *NOT* the God of the Bible!

THE TRUTH CONCERNING GOD

Study the Scriptures for yourself. God is *much more **loving** and **powerful*** than we have been led to believe.

"God is love" and *"love **never fails"*** (I John 4:8; I Corinthians 13:8).

It is God's will that *all* mankind be saved, and He does *all* that He wills to do. The Scriptures teach us that He will in fact reconcile ***"all things"*** unto Himself (Colossians 1:20).

God is *loving* and *powerful* enough to accomplish all of His purposes – including saving *every* person.

BETTER GOOD NEWS!

The Gospel of our Lord and Savior Jesus Christ is truly better *"good news"* than many of us could ever have imagined! It is *far more glorious* than most would ever have us believe!

Harold Lovelace
(Adapted)

Appendix 32

SELECT SHORT QUOTES

There is no difficulty that enough love will not conquer; … No door that enough love will not open; No gulf that enough love will not bridge; No wall that enough love will not throw down; No sin that enough love will not redeem …

Emmet Fox (1886-1951)
Love

If I were Jesus Christ, I would save Judas.

Victor Hugo (1802-1885)
Life (page 154)

God forbid that I should limit the time of acquiring faith to the present life. In the depth of the Divine mercy there may be opportunity to win it in the future.

Martin Luther (1483-1546)
Letter to Hanseu Von Rechenberg
1522

God will not conquer evil by crushing it under-foot – any god of man's idea could do that – but by conquest of heart over heart, of life over life, of life over death, of love over all.

Justice requires that sin should be put an end to.

George MacDonald (1824-1905)
Wisdom To Live By

I am so tried by the things said about God. I understand God's patience with the wicked, but I do wonder how He can be so patient with the pious.

George MacDonald (1824-1905)
The Elect Lady

God created all things and mankind for the sake of manifesting His glory. Today, believers are manifesting little somethings of Christ. But one day, all things shall manifest Christ because the whole universe shall be filled with Him. In creating all things, God desires that all things will manifest Christ.

Watchman Nee
God's Plan and the Overcomers

The notion that a creature born imperfect, nay, born with impulses to evil not of his own generating, and which he could not help having, a creature to whom the true face of God was never presented, and by whom it never could have been seen, should be thus condemned, is as loathsome a lie against God as could find place in a heart too undeveloped to understand what justice is.

George MacDonald (1824-1905)
Justice

The notion of the popular creed, (*i.e.*, that God is in the Bible detailing the story of His own defeat, how sin has proved too strong for Him), seems wholly unfounded. Assuredly the Bible is not the story of sin, deepening into eternal ruin, of God's Son, worsted in His utmost effort. It is from the opening to the close the story of grace stronger than sin – of life victorious over every form of death – of God triumphant over evil.

Thomas Allin (1835-1908)
Christ Triumphant

In the perspective of the future we have stopped short of the far-off goal, and explained the finale of God's purposes by the episode or process on the way thereto.

A.E. Saxby
God in Creation, Redemption, Judgment and Consummation
1966

I believe that God is good. No thought I have ever had of God is better than God actually is ... I have never overestimated how good God is because God's goodness overflows far beyond the limits of human understanding.

Brian McLaren
The Last Word and the Word After That (page xi)
(2005)

If Christ has died for you, you can never be lost. God will not punish twice for one thing. If God punished Christ for your sins He will not punish you ... How can God be just if he punished Christ, the substitute, and then man himself afterwards?

Charles H. Spurgeon (1834-1892)
Cited by Gregg Strawbridge, *Power in the Blood*

Yes, He is holy; yes, He is a righteous Judge. But He always exercises these attributes within the framework of His mercy and grace.

Charles Stanley
A Gift of Love
2001, Page 15

Grace is amazing because it is limitless. God's grace can never be exhausted. Regardless of the vileness or number of our sins, His grace is always sufficient. It can never be depleted; it can never be measured. He always gives His grace in fullness.

Charles Stanley
A Gift of Love
2001, Page 9

When Paul uses the expression "many," he is not intending to delimit the denotation. The scope of "many" must be the same as the "all men" of verses 12 and 18. He uses "many" here, as in verse 19, for the purpose of contrasting more effectively "one" and "many," singularity and plurality – it was the trespass of one … but "many" died as a result.

John Murray
Epistle of Paul to the Romans

"For God hath concluded them all in unbelief, that He might have mercy upon all" (Romans 11:32).

God is in all this – every bit of it – the evil as well as the good. He shuts us up in unbelief, that He may have mercy on us, so when folks walk Satan's way, they are being taken that way by a God who has designs of mercy on them.

Norman P. Grubb (1895-1993)
Notes from Norman

If but one soul were to remain in the power of the devil, death, or hell, to all endless eternity, then the devil, death, and hell would have something to boast of against God. Thus death would not be entirely swallowed up in victory, but always keep something of his sting, and hell would ever more be able to make a scorn of those who would say, "O hell, where is, your victory?"

Paul Seigvolck
The Everlasting Gospel
1753

Shall he say "Forgive seventy times seven," and Himself not forgive except in this short life? Shall He command us to "overcome evil with good," and Himself, the Almighty, be overcome of evil? Shall He judge those who leave the captives unvisited, and Himself leave captives in a worse prison for ever unvisited? Does He not again and again appeal to our own natural feelings of mercy, as witnessing "how much more" we may expect a larger mercy from our "Father which is in Heaven?"

Andrew Jukes (1815-1901)
The Restitution of All Things
1867, page 94

The salvation of the whole human race is what God proposed in the creation. It is what Christ came into the world to effect, and for the accomplishment of which he was given all needed power in heaven and earth. To this end he died the death of the cross, and thus tasted death for every man; and I submit that such self-sacrificing love cannot suddenly cool, or readily give over to endless torment souls for which it thus willingly suffered. I should be ashamed of myself, if, believing in God and in Christ, I still feared their ultimate failure in this great work of redemption, whose history fills the Bible.

Thomas J. Sawyer (1804-1899)
Endless Punishment In the Very Words of Its Advocates
1880

The monstrous, unscriptural idea that men are tormented in death, before they are brought to judgment, is so revolting to every sense of justice that its absence from the Word of God is one evidence of divine inspiration. Even among civilized men a prisoner is not punished before he is judged. If the men of Adam's day have been tormented ever since and will suffer until the day of judgment, when they will be tried, then God's judgment is a farce and there is no reason for a resurrection.

A.E. Knoch (1874-1965)
All in All: The Goal of the Universe
Page 30, 31

Some of our young people are seen with T-shirts with the inscription: "Be patient ... God isn't finished with me yet." Maybe God is not finished with any of us yet. If He is Lord of both the living and the dead, then can we not hope that His saving work goes on after death? Certainly, a clearer picture of Christ in judgment and grace will prove highly convincing. Someday all will see Him, know of His lavish generosity and therefore extend hope for all.

Randy Klassen
What Does the Bible Really Say About Hell? (page 103)
(2001)

To believe that anyone goes into the Lake of Fire to bear that punishment again for sin is actually to diminish the work of Calvary and to detract from the perfect atonement of the cross, making it without effect and altogether unnecessary. Hence, we must view the Lake of Fire as being something other than retributive; and our only alternative is that the Lake of Fire is remedial ...

It becomes morally impossible for all things to be both subject to Jesus Christ and yet sinfully rebellious against Him at the same time.

Charles P. Schmitt
The Unending Triumph of Jesus Christ

"And, having made peace through the blood of His cross, by Him to reconcile all things unto Himself; by Him, I say, whether they be things in earth, or things in heaven" (Colossians 1:20).

If by that Cross all things in the heavens are to be reconciled, and infinite peace is to follow, I dare trust it, notwithstanding all my sin and all my weakness. By the way of that Cross I am reconciled to God, and through it I find rest, infinite, eternal, undying. At last my rest shall be rest with the WHOLE CREATION, for the cosmic order will be restored through the mystery of God's suffering as revealed in the Cross.

G. Campbell Morgan (1863-1945)
The Cross and the Ages to Come
"The Presbyterian," June 1932

"To wit, that God was in Christ, reconciling the world unto Himself, not imputing their trespasses unto them; and hath committed unto us the word of reconciliation" (II Corinthians 5:19).

The truth is most blessed and comforting that *"God was in Christ reconciling the world unto Himself."* This is *"glad tidings"* or *"good news"* indeed!

There is no "angry Heaven," whose wrath must be appeased, and whose favor must be purchased; but a loving Father, who Himself is working to win back the prodigal to the arms that are ever stretched out to receive Him, and the heart that has never ceased to love him.

Arthur P. Adams
The Atonement
1885

The work that put sinners right with God is complete. The old hymn tells the truth: "Jesus Paid It All!" We cannot add anything to this saving work that Jesus has accomplished. We cannot improve on it. We cannot supplement it. We cannot make it shine any brighter. We cannot do anything to make God love us more than He already does ...

Nothing we can ever learn, nothing that we will ever do, nothing we might ever experience can contribute anything whatsoever to the work that sets us right with God. That work is the perfect doing and the perfect dying of Jesus Christ, our substitute and representative. Jesus completed the work. God accepted it and stamped it with His endorsement. The work that sets us right with God is finished. It is finished! ...

The gospel is the "good news" that God has set sinners right with Himself through Jesus Christ.

Edward William Fudge
The Great Rescue: The Story of God's Amazing Grace
2002, page 86

The wages of sin is death (Romans 6:23).

Is death eternal in any sense?

If *death* really means *eternal life* in some really nasty place, or eternal *destruction* from the presence of God, and if Jesus paid (past tense really wouldn't work here) the penalty for sin (Hebrews 2:9), how is it that Jesus is now at the right hand of the Father (Acts 7:55-56)?

If *death* really means death (the cessation of life), and it means *forever dead*, how is it that Jesus is now at the right hand of the Father (Romans 8:34; 6:9)?

How can death be *"swallowed up in victory"* (I Corinthians 15:54), and *"be no more"* (Revelation 21:4), if a single created being remains in its grip?

If, on the other hand, death does mean the cessation of life (Ezekiel 18:20), and Jesus has paid the penalty IN FULL for all men (I John 2:2), abolishing death (II Timothy 1:10), and when the last of mankind bows the knee and confesses Jesus (Philippians 2:10-11) – which thing can only be done by the Holy Spirit (I Corinthians 12:3) – and receives salvation and immortality (Romans 10:10; I Corinthians 15:53-54) – which only Jesus possesses (I Timothy 6:16) – will not *"the last enemy,"* death, truly be *"swallowed up in victory"* (I Corinthians 15:54) and *"be no more"* Revelation 21:4)?

Is this not Father's will (I Timothy 2:4)? Shall He not accomplish all of His will (Isaiah 46:10)?

Joel Olson (1955-)
Amarillo, TX

Bibliography

Abbott-Smith, George, *Manual Greek Lexicon of the New Testament,* T & T Clark, 1950

Adams, Arthur P., *The Atonement,* The Spirit of the Word, 1885

Allen, Stuart, *Resurrection and the Purpose of the Ages*, Berean Publishing Trust, 1957

Allin, Thomas, *Christ Triumphant*, Scriptures Studies Concern, 1949

Anderson, Sir Robert, *Human Destiny*, Hodder and Stoughton, 1895

Ballinger, Tom L., *Plainer Words Online,* HeavenDwellers.com

Barclay, William, *A Spiritual Autobiography*, Eerdmans, 1977

Barnes, Albert, *Practical Sermons,* 1855

Barnhart, Robert K., *Barnhart's Concise Dictionary of Etymology*, Harper Collins, 1995

Blunt, J.S., *Dictionary of Theology,* n.d.

Bullinger, E.W., *Critical Lexicon and Concordance of the English and Greek New Testament,* Zondervan, 1975

Bullinger, E.W., *The Rich Man and Lazarus*, Eyre & Spottiswoode, 1911

Cox, Samuel, *Salvator Mundi, or Is Christ the Saviour of All Men?* Kegan Paul, 1877

Crim, Keith R., George A. Butterick, *Interpreter's Dictionary of the Bible,* Abingdon Press, 1976

Darby, J.N., *The Hopes of the Church*, F. Baisler, 1841

De Haan, Mart, *Radio Bible Class Newsletter*, November 2006

Donnegan, James, *A New Greek and English Lexicon*, Hilliard, Gray & Company, 1839

Ellicott, Charles John, *Ellicott's Commentary on the Whole Bible,* Zondervan, 1957

Evely, Bob, *Grace Evangel Newsletter*, 2003

Farrar, Frederic William, *Mercy and Judgment*, Macmillan and Co, 1882

Farrar, Frederic William, *The Wider Hope*, Macmillan and Co, 1890

Fudge, Edward William, *The Great Rescue, The Story of God's Amazing Grace*, Leafwood Publishing, 2002

Gavazzoni, John R., *The Cup of God's Wrath*, Lighthouse Library, 2006

Grubb, Norman P., *Notes From Norman,* NormanGrubb.com

Hanson, J.W., *The Greek Word Aion,* North-Western, 1875

Hartman, L.F. *Encyclopedic Dictionary of the Bible*, McGraw-Hill, 1963

Hastings, James, *Hastings Dictionary of the New Testament*, Baker Book House, 1973

Hawtin, G.R., *Creation, Redemption, and the Restitution of All Things,* Modern Press Limited, n.d.

Hurley, Loyal, *The Outcome of Infinite Grace*, Bible Student's Press, 2007

Jacobson, V.E., *Fifteen Bombs That Sank My Theological Ship*, Grace and Truth Chapel

Jukes, Andrew, *The Restitution of All Things*, Longmans, Green, 1867

Kennedy, John, *Word Stems, A Dictionary*, Soho Press, 1996

Kingsley, Charles, *Endless Torments Unscriptural,* 1865

Kirk, Joseph E., *The Good News Gospel* Concordant Publishing Concern, n.d.

Kirk, Joseph E., *Will All Mankind Be Constituted Righteous Through Jesus Christ?* Savior of All Fellowship, n.d.

Kissinger, Thomas, *The Glory of God and the Honor of Kings,* n.d.

Klassen, Randy, *What Does the Bible Really Say About Hell?,* Pandora Press, 2001

Knoch, A.E., *All in All: The Goal of the Universe,* Concordant Publishing Concern, 1978

Lehman, Frederick M., *The Love of God*, 1917

Liddell, Henry G., Robert Scott, *Liddell and Scott's Greek-English Lexicon*, Harper & Brothers, 1896

Luther, Martin, *A Letter to Hanseu Von Rechenberg*, 1522

MacDonald, George, *The Elect Lady*, 1888

MacDonald, George, *Wisdom to Live By*, 1885

MacDonald, George, *Justice*, n.d.

McLaren, Brian D., *The Last Word and the Word After That*, Jossey-Bass, 2005

Mealand, William, *Unsearchable Riches*, 1917

Morgan, G. Campbell, *God's Methods With Men*, n.d.

Morgan, G. Campbell, *The Cross and the Ages to Come*, The Presbyterian, 1932

Murray, John, *The Epistle of Paul to the Romans*, Eerdmans, 1965

Nee, Watchman, *God's Plan and the Overcomers*, Christian Fellowship Publishers, 1977

Newell, William R., *Paul's Gospel*, Gospel Tract Distributors, n.d.

Orr, James, *International Standard Bible Encyclopedia*, Eerdmans, 1983

Partridge, Eric, *Origins, A Short Etymological Dictionary of Modern English*, Greenwich House, 1983

Pilkington, Clyde L. Jr., *Bible Student's Notebook*, Pilkington & Sons, 1989-2006

Sawyer, Thomas J., *Endless Punishment in the Very Words of Its Advocates*, Universalist Publishing House, 1880

Saxby, A.E., God *in Creation, Redemption, Judgment and Consummation*, London, England, 1922, reprinted by Bible Student's Press, 2010

Schleusner, John, *Novus Thesaurus Philologico-Criticus*, 1829

Schmitt, Charles P., *The Unending Triumph of Jesus Christ*, n.d.

Scofield, C.I., *Scofield Reference Bible*, Oxford University Press, 1909, 1917

Seigvolck, Paul, *The Everlasting Gospel*, 1753

Sellers, Otis, *The Study of Human Destiny*, The Word of Truth, 1943

Short, Robert L., *Short Mediations on the Bible and Peanuts*, Westminster John Knox Press, 1991

Skeat, Walter, *The Concise Dictionary of English Etymology*, 1882, Wordsworth reprint, 1993

Stanley, Charles, *A Gift of Love*, Thomas Nelson, 2001

Strawbridge, Gregg, *The Power of the Blood*, n.d.

Strong, James, *Strong's Exhaustive Concordance of the Bible*, Hinderickson

Talbott, Thomas, *The Inescapable Love of God*, Universal Publishers, 1999

Thayer, J.H., *Thayer's Greek-English Lexicon of the New Testament*, Baker, 1995

Thomas, W.H., *The Presbyterian*, 1932

Vincent, Marvin, *Word Studies in the New Testament*, Macdonald Publishing Company, 1967

Vine, W.E., *Vine's Expository Dictionary*, Revell, 1981

Webster, Noah, *An American Dictionary of the English Language*, 1828, reprint by F.A.C.E.

Weekly, Ernest, *An Etymological Dictionary of Modern English*, 1921, Dover reprint 1967

Welch, Charles H., *An Alphabetical Analysis*, Berean Publishing Trust, 1955

Wilhelm, Charles J., *Biblical Dyslexia*, Xulon Press, 2004

Wolf, William J., *The Almost Chosen People*, Doubleday & Company, 1959

Young, Robert, *Analytical Concordance to the Bible*, Henderickson

Your Part

Now that you have read this book, it's your turn.

If the truths presented here have helped you, don't let these truths die in your hands.

Please write to us and let us know your thoughts concerning its content.

Consider assisting us in getting this book into the hands of those who would be encouraged and strengthened by its message:

- Recommend it to your friends and loved ones.
- Order additional copies to give as gifts.
- Keep extra copies on hand to loan to others.

If you have not read the author's other works, order them today.

We would be honored to have your fellowship in getting this book freely to those who hunger spiritually. We have daily opportunities to send it to pastors, Sunday school teachers, Bible college professors and students, Bible class teachers, and prisoners.

Enjoy Books?

Visit us at:

www.StudyShelf.com

Over the years we have often been asked to recommend books. The requests come from believers who longed for material with substance. Study Shelf™ is a collection of books which are, in our opinion, the very best in print. Many of these books are "unknown" to the members of the Body of Christ at large, and most are not available at your local "Christian" bookstore.

You Can:

Read

A wealth of articles from past issues of the *Bible Student's Notebook* ™

Purchase

Rare and hard to find books, booklets, leaflets, Bibles, etc. in our 24/7 on-line store.

Do You Subscribe
to the

Bible

Student's

Notebook™*?*

This is a periodical that ...
- Promotes the study of the Bible
- Encourages the growth of the believer in grace
- Supports the role of the family patriarch
- Is dedicated to the recovery of truth that has too long been hidden under the veils of traditionalism, prejudice, misunderstanding and fear
- Is not connected with any "Movement," "Organization," "Mission," or separate body of believers, but is sent forth to and for all saints.

The ***Bible Student's Notebook***™ is published weekly (52 times a year).

Subscribe Today!

<u>Electronic Version</u> *(e-Mailed to you!)*
Less than *20¢* per weekly issue!

1 Year Electronic Subscription – *52 weekly issues (#8298)* .... $10.^{00}
2 Year Electronic Subscription – *52 weekly issues (#8294)* .... $20.^{00}

<u>Printed Version</u> *(Mailed to you!)*
Less than *$1.$^{00}* per weekly issue!

½ Year Printed Subscription – *26 weekly issues (#8297)* .... $25.^{00}
1 Year Printed Subscription – *52 weekly issues (#8296)* .... $50.^{00}

Bible Student's Notebook™
PO Box 265 Windber, PA 15963
www.BibleStudentsNotebook.com
1-800-784-6010

Other Great Titles Available on the subject of THE SALVATION OF ALL and Related Themes:

All in All: The Goal of the Universe (#6269) by A.E. Knoch. (1874-1965). 222 pages, PB.

Ancient History of Universalism (#1926) by Hosea Ballou. 326 pages, PB.

At The End of the Ages: The Abolition of Hell (#3331) by Bob Evely. 171 pages, PB.

Bible Proofs of Universal Salvation (#2895) by J.W. Hanson. 107 pages, PB.

Bible Student's Notebook: Salvation OF ALL (SET) (#8302) by Clyde L. Pilkington, Jr. 52 pages, 8½" X 11", NB.

Bible Threatenings Explained: Or *Passages of Scripture Sometimes Quoted to Prove Endless Punishment Shown to Teach Consequences of Limited Duration* (#2965) by J.W. Hanson. 209 pages, PB.

Christ Triumphant, Or Universalism Asserted (#2264) by Thomas Allin. 327 pages, PB.

Death, Resurrection, Immortality (#2052) by Joseph E. Kirk. 111 pages, PB.

Destined for Salvation: God's Promise to Save Everyone (#3173) by Kalen Fristad. 157 pages, PB.

Endless Punishment: In the Very Words of Its Advocates (#7888) by Thomas J. Sawyer (1804-1899). 145 pages, NB.

Eonian: Everlasting or Age-Lasting? (#7673) complied by G.H. Todd. 47 pages, BK.

Eternal Torment, or Universal Reconciliation (#5601) by A.E. Knoch (1874- 1965). 51 pages, BK.

Every Knee Shall Bow: The Case for Christian Universalism (#4510) by Thomas Allin & Mark T. Chamberlain. 123 pages, PB.

God Does Not Foreclose: The Universal Promise of Salvation (#5202) by David L. Watson. 160 pages, PB.

God's Eonian Purpose (#3554) by Adlai Loudy. 383 pages, PB.

Greek Word AION - AIONIOS, Translated Everlasting - Eternal, The (#6562) by John Wesley Hanson. 79 pages, BK.

HELL, or "Pure from the blood of all men" (#6248) by Charles H. Welch. 57 pages, BK.

Hope Beyond Hell: The Righteous Purpose Of God's Judgment. (#4225) by Gerry Beauchemin. 247 pages, PB.

Humanity in the Arms of a Loving Savior (#4508) by James T. Burson. 68 pages, BK.

If God Could Save Everyone, WOULD HE?? (#4113) by Dr. Stephen E. Jones. 36 pages, BK.

Inescapable Love of God, The (#1814) by Thomas Talbott. 223 pages, PB.

Legend of Hell, The: An Examination of the Idea of Everlasting Punishment (#2235) by Percy Dearmer (1867-1936). 144 pages, 8½" X 11", NB.

Martin Zender Goes To Hell (#6494) by Martin Zender. 78 pages, PB.

Modern History of Universalism, The (#2079) by Thomas Whittemore (1800-1861). 458 pages, HB.

One Purpose of God, The: *An Answer to the Doctrine of Eternal Punishment* (#1816) by J. Bonda. 278 pages, PB.

Outcome of Infinite Grace (#6388) by Loyal F. Hurley. 62 pages, BK.

The Really Bad Thing About Free Will (#2250) by Martin Zender. 80 pages, PB.

Restitution of All Things (#3286) by Andrew Jukes. 194 pages, PB.

Restitution of All Things, The (#5175) by G.R. Hawtin. 47 pages, BK.

Restoration Of All Things, The: or Vindication of the Goodness and Grace of God. A (#2084) by Jeremiah White. 88 pages, 8½" x 11" PB.

Resurrection Of The Body, The (#1375) by E.W. Bullinger. 16 Pages, BK.

Rich Man and Lazarus, The (#7495) by Alan Burns. 30 pages, BK.

Rich Man and Lazarus, The (#6298) by Otis Q Sellers. 48 pages, BK.

Rich Man and Lazarus, The: *The Intermediate State* (#3127) by E.W. Bullinger. 64 pages, PB.

Salvation of the Unbeliever (#9125) by A.E. Knoch (1874-1965). 20 pages, BK.

Salvator Mundi: Is Christ the Saviour of All Men? (#6219) by Samuel Cox (1826-1893). 256 pages, PB.

Saviour of All Mankind (#3053) Compilation. 48 pages, BK.

Spirits In Prison, The (#1450) by E.W. Bullinger. A Study of (I Peter 3:17 – 4:6). 29 pages, BK.

Time and Eternity: A Biblical Study (#4209) by G.T. Stevenson. 76 pages, BK

Treatise on Atonement: The Final Reconciliation Of All Men (#1733) by Hosea Ballou. (8" x 11") PB.

Two Studies on Heaven and Hell (#7979) by A.E. Knoch (1874-1965). 27 pages, BK.

Union: or A Treatise of the Consanguinity and Affinity Between Christ and His Church (#2085) James Relly (1722-1778). 42 pages, 8½" x 11" PB.

Universal Restoration (#4134) by Elhanan Winchester (1751-1797). 72 pages, PB.

Universal Salvation? The Current Debate (#3591) by Thomas Talbott and others. 291 pages, PB.

Voice To Universalists (#2999) by Hosea Ballou. 8" x 11", PB.

What Does the Bible Say About Hell? *Wrestling with the Traditional View* (#1815) by Randy Klassen. 144 pages, PB.

DAILY E-MAIL GOODIES™

Do you receive our
Daily E-mail Goodies™?

These are free daily e-mails that contain short quotes, articles, and studies on Biblical themes.

These are the original writings of Clyde L. Pilkington, Jr., as well as gleanings from other authors.

Here is what our readers are saying:

"Profound! Comforting! Calming! Wonderful!" – **NC**

*"I am glad to be getting the **Daily E-mail Goodies** – keep 'em coming."* – **IN**

*"The **Daily E-mail Goodies** continue to bless my heart! ... They provide plenty of food for thought."* – **IL**

*"I really appreciate the **Goodies!**"* – **VA**

*"Your **Daily E-mail Goodies** are making me aware of authors whose names I don't even know."* – **GA**

Request to be added to our free
Daily E-mail Goodies™

If you would like to be added to the mailing list, e-mail us at:

Goodies@StudyShelf.com

www.URQA.com

Universal Reconciliation

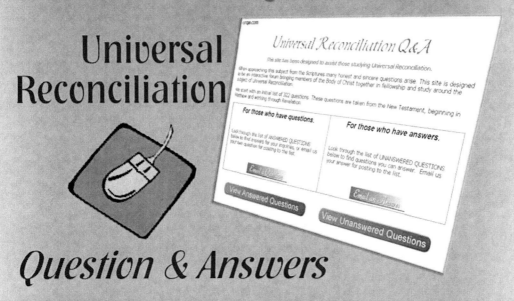

Question & Answers

A website designed to assist those studying Universal Reconciliation.

When approaching this subject from the Scriptures many honest and sincere questions arise. This site is designed to be an interactive forum bringing members of the Body of Christ together in fellowship and study around the subject of Universal Reconciliation.

We start with an initial list of 322 questions. These questions are taken from the New Testament, beginning in Matthew and working through Revelation.

For those who have questions:

Look through a list of ANSWERED QUESTIONS to find answers for your inquiries, or email us your own question for posting to the list.

For those who have answers:

Look through a list of UNANSWERED QUESTIONS to find questions you can answer. Email us your answers for posting to the list.

Stop by www.urqa.com

Today!

Believer's Warfare, The: Wearing the Armor of Light in the Darkness of this World

(#7000) The believer is in the middle of an ancient spiritual warfare that is as old as mankind. The battle itself, although intense, is not complicated. It is not a process of spiritual hoop-jumping. Indeed it is simple. The Believer's Warfare surveys a few key passages of Scripture to reveal God's sure plan of victory in the life of His saints. ISBN: 9781934251003 – 48 pages, BK.

Bible Student's Notebook, The (VOLUMES)

The Bible Student's Notebook is a periodical dedicated to the: – Promotion of Bible study – Encouragement of the believer's growth in grace – Support of the role of family patriarch – Recovery of truth that has too long been hidden under the veils of traditionalism, prejudice, misunderstanding and fear. The Bible Student's Notebook is not connected with any "Church," "Movement," "Organization," "Society," "Mission," or separate body of believers, but is sent forth to and for all of God's saints. Available in Paperback Volumes.

Church in Ruins, The: Brief Thoughts on II Timothy

(#3325) This brief survey of Paul's last epistle will reveal that, while almost 2000 years have transpired, the condition of the church has remained the same, and indeed has worsened in accordance with Paul's warning to Timothy. This book is not a call for a re-awakening of "the church," because it is apparent that this is not Father's plan. Rather, it is a call to individual men – men whose place in the Christian religious system has left them empty, stagnant and restless – to awaken to Father's call to be His faithful servant and stand outside of that system to look for other faithful men as well. – 128 pages, PB.

Due Benevolence: A Study of Biblical Sexuality

(#3775) Think you have read all that there is on the subject of sexuality from the Bible? Think again! Religious moralist have taken the wonderful gifts of human beauty and sexuality, and made them something dirty and sinful. Much is at stake regarding truth, as well as the nature and character of God Himself. A groundbreaking work providing:

- A refreshingly honest and uninhibited look at sexuality.
- A breath of fresh air from the religious and Victorian mentality.
- A daring and valuable glimpse at the wonderful light just outside sexuality's prison-cell door.

– 220 pages, PB.

Heaven's Embassy: The Divine Plan & Purpose of the Home

(#5675) The home is central to all of God's dealings with man throughout the course of time. It is His Divine "institution" and "organization" upon the earth, and for the believer, it is the Embassy of Heaven. An embassy is "the residence or office of an ambassador." Since the believer is an ambassador of the Lord Jesus Christ (II Corinthians 5:14-21), his home is thus the Divine Embassy of heavenly ministry. Pauline ministry is centered in the homes of believers. This is even the true sphere of the Body of Christ; for this reason our apostle speaks of "church in thy house." This book doesn't focus upon  the external specifics of the ministry of Heaven's Embassy (such as hospitality); that will be saved for another volume. Instead, it looks at the inner-workings of the Embassy itself; focusing upon its very nature and internal purpose and function. – 250 pages, PB.

I Choose! Living Life to Its Fullest

(#4120) Forty-Eight Daily Thoughts on Divine Life. You are alive! Yet not just alive, but alive with the very life of God! Don't allow your "What if …" imaginations of the past or the future to lay claim to the present that God has given you. Allow the objective, unchanging truth of who God has made you in the Lord Jesus Christ to transform your mind and life as you take this spiritual journey of "I Choose." – 192 pages, PB.

Nothing Will Be Lost! The Truth About God's Good News

(#3750) This is an abridgement of the larger work The Salvation of All. It is designed as a give-away edition, with quantity pricing available. – 88 pages, PB.

The Outsiders: God's Called-Out Ones
A Biblical Look at the Church – God's Ecclesia

(#4125) In 1995, after sixteen years of being in the "pastorate" the author walked away. He left the "religious system" by resigning from the very "church" and "ministry" he had formed. In many ways this work is a testament to these actions. This testimony was thirty years in the making – the results of a spiritual journey that the author found to be common to other saints scattered throughout the world and across history. This is an opportunity to explain why some who love the Lord no longer "go to church." It does not seek to persuade others to do something different; but rather to be simply who and what they already are "in Him." This is an uncovering of the truth of the church, and an encouragement for the members of His Body to enjoy the position and standing "in Christ" that they already possess, realizing that they are truly *"complete in Him"* (Colossians 2:10), that He alone is their Life (Colossians 3:4), and that His Life is full of freedom (Galatians 5:1). ISBN: 9781934251614 – 128 pages, PB.

Plowboy's Bible, The : God's Word for Common Man

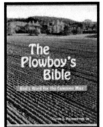

(#4425) Shocking conclusions from the man that brought you The King James Bible Song. This book represents years of study and a significant change in understanding. Raised on and trained in a "King James Only" position, most of the author's teaching ministry was centered on the defense of the KJV. He had early associations with major proponents of this position and their followers. He actively taught classes and seminars on the subject of Bible versions. For many years he distributed thousands of books from a collection of over 100 different titles in support of the KJV position. Here he shares what he has come to see that has caused him to completely abandon his former position. – 254 pages, PB.

Salvation Of ALL, The: Creation's Final Destination
(A Biblical Look at Universal Reconciliation)

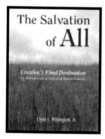

(#7001) The Gospel of our Lord and Savior, Jesus Christ is truly better "Good News" than we could ever have imagined. It is far more glorious than religion would ever have us believe. The Salvation of All is a book about a "Good News" that will reach its final goal in the salvation of all mankind. – 262 pages, PB.

Suffering: God's Forgotten Gift

Two gifts given to the believer are mentioned by Paul in Philippians 1:29. The first is *"to believe on Him."* This is a glorious gift. Every believer has been given this gift from God. Those who possess it may not even fully recognize it as a gift from Him, but indeed faith is God's wonderful gift to us. Faith is a rich gift from God, but there is also another gift from God to the believer mentioned by Paul in Philippians 1:29 that is equally as glorious. The second gift is *"also to suffer for His sake."* This, too, is a glorious gift. Every believer has been given this gift from God as well, but those who possess it  often do not fully recognize it for what it is. Indeed, suffering for His sake similarly is God's wonderful gift to us. Paul teaches us to embrace this second gift as well as we do the first! – 100 pages PB.

TO ORDER:

visit: *ClydePilkington.com*

or

call Toll Free: 1-800-784-6010

CPSIA information can be obtained at www.ICGtesting.com
Printed in the USA
BVOW061535290313

316843BV00004B/79/P